Saturn Through the Ages:
Between Time and Eternity

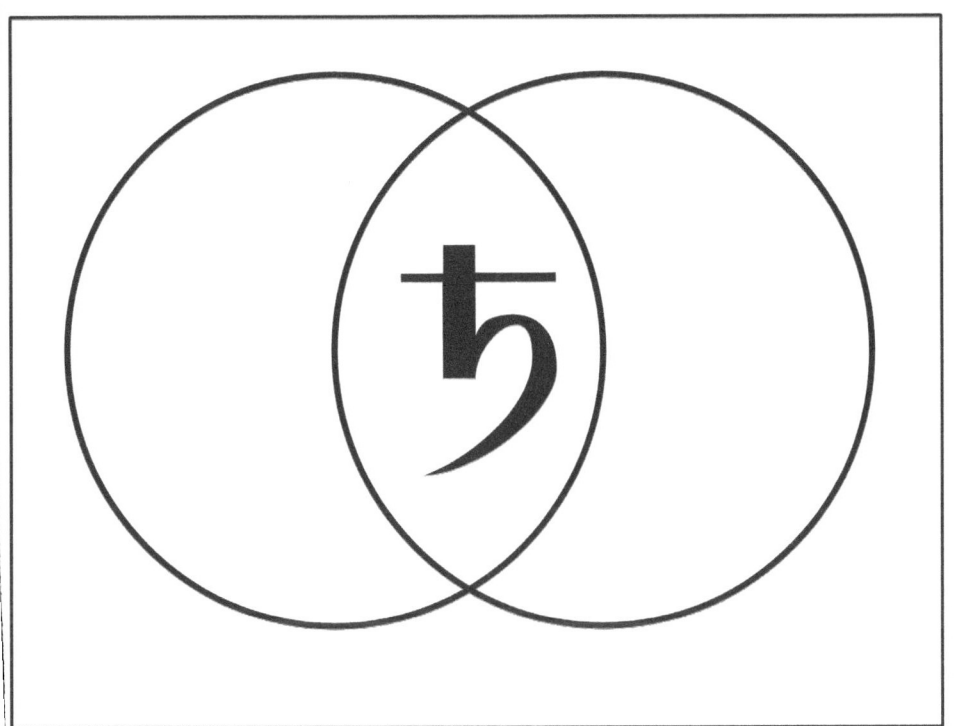

Charles Obert

Almuten Press

Published and printed in the United States of America

By Almuten Press

3507 Taylor Street NE, Minneapolis, MN 55418

©2019 by Charles Obert

All rights reserved. No part of this publication may be reproduced stored in or introduced into a retrieval system, or transmitted, in any form or by any means (electronic, mechanical, photocopying, recording or otherwise), without the prior written permission of both the copyright owner and the above publisher of this book.

The scanning, uploading, and distribution of this book via the Internet or via any other means without the permission of the publisher is illegal and punishable by law. Please purchase only authorized electronic editions and do not participate in or encourage electronic piracy of copyrighted materials. Your support of the author's rights is appreciated.

ISBN-13: 978-0-9864187-4-7

Dedication

It is with great pleasure that I dedicate this book to my daughter, Eve Patrice Obert.

Acknowledgements

I want to thank all the people who took the time to review and and give me feedback on earlier drafts of this book. In alphabetical order: Rebecca Bihr, Heather Figearo, Nina Gryphon, Jane Littrell, Rita Navroth, Hitomi Oshita, Allison Simon, Madeliene Youngstrom, Darleen Yuna.

Also by Charles Obert

Introduction to Traditional Natal Astrology: A Guide for Modern Astrologers
A user-friendly introduction to the basic concepts and techniques of traditional astrology. Instructions are given for evaluating planetary strength and conditions, and a full outline of traditional chart interpretation.

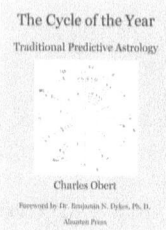

Using Dignities In Astrology
An in-depth study of the traditional system of dignities and debilities for weighing up the condition of planets and points in a chart. Major and minor dignities, debilities, accidental dignities, how to weigh and combine all of the different factors.

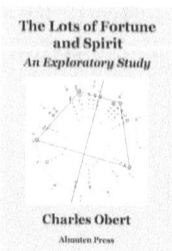

The Cycle of the Year: Traditional Predictive Astrology
The techniques used annually in traditional predictive astrology, including distributions through the bounds, profections and solar returns.

Foreword by Benjamin N. Dykes, Ph. D.

The Lots of Fortune and Spirit: An Exploratory Study
A practical study of how the two main Lots, Fortune and Spirit, actually work in practice.

PDF versions are available at **https://studentofastrology.com**

Table of Contents

Introduction..10
The Chesterton Test..13

Part One: Historical Survey................................14
Vettius Valens, Anthology...15
Firmicus Maternus, Mathesis...21
Abu Ma'shar, The Great Introduction..............................23
Al-Biruni..26
Avraham Ibn-Ezra, The Beginning of Wisdom................29
Bonatti, Book of Astronomy..31
William Lilly: Christian Astrology....................................35

The Meanings of Saturn in Traditional Astrology....43
Transition Astrologers..49
Raphael Guide to Astrology..50
Sepharial, The Manual of Astrology................................52

The Old and New Cosmos...54
Max Heindel..67
Llewellyn George..70
Charles E O Carter...72
The Only Way to Learn Astrology....................................74
Ronald Davison..77
Isabel Hickey..80
Zipporah Dobyns..83
Liz Greene..86

Steven Forrest - The Inner Sky...93
James Hillman and Archetypal Astrology..............................96
Current Archetypal Astrology...102
Uranian Astrology & its Descendants......................................105
Alfred Witte - Uranian Astrology...105
Reinhold Ebertin - Cosmobiology..107
David Cochrane - Vibrational Astrology.................................109

The Contribution of Modern Astrology...................111

Part Two: The Eternal Law..................................116
Introduction..116
Platonic Model of the Universe..117
Eternal Law...123
Eternal Moral Law..129
Saturn and the Golden Age..135
Cycles of Time and Eternity..139
Saturn and Ouranos..146
Consistency in Astrology...149
The Sphere of Saturn and Astrology...150
Living in Two Worlds..152

Part Three - Essays on Saturn Themes................155
Introduction..155
Balance..156
Tradition..168
Uranus and Saturn..170
Saturn and Pluto...175

    Benefic and Malefic..179
    Evil..182
    Fortune...189
    Old Age...197
    Suffering...202
    Death...206
    Fear of God...209
    Humility..211

Final Thoughts...213

Appendix..215
Science: the Changed Meaning of the Word...........215
Plato and Reincarnation: the Myth of Er................223

Bibliography..245

Introduction

Many astrologers have their favorite planets, the ones they resonate to the most, the ones they find the most interesting. Typically it is a planet that is particularly strong or prominent in their own chart.

Mine is Saturn.

My rising sign is Capricorn. The ruling planet, Saturn, is exalted in Libra in my tenth house by whole sign, aspecting the Ascendant by a tight square. In traditional astrology the ruler of the Ascendant represents the person. In traditional astrology sense I am Saturn. I have written more about Saturn than all of the other six traditional planets put together.

Purpose

The purpose of this book is to recover the full traditional meaning of Saturn, and to recover a living context within which that full traditional meaning makes living sense. The meaning of Saturn relies on its context.

The pivotal meaning of Saturn, that which everything else hinges on, comes from it being the outermost planet, on the border between the worlds of time and eternity. That is the key to the full riches of Saturn's meanings, and I want to recover that meaning and context in this book.

Part One explores the full meaning of the planet Saturn through history. Part Two gives a living context for that meaning to make sense in our modern world. Part Three explores and develops some specific aspects of Saturn's meaning.

Introduction

Outline

Part One: Historical Survey. The purpose of the first section, the historical survey, is to document the diifferent meanings attributed to Saturn throughout the history of Western astrology. You will find that through all of the traditional writers, from Vettius Valens in the second century to William Lilly in the seventeenth century, the meanings attributed to Saturn stay quite remarkably consistent.

It is not until the modern era, especially from the early twentieth century and later, that we see significant changes in the meanings attributed to Saturn. The differences in meaning of Saturn go together with a significant shift in overall worldview, the assumptions we make when we look out at the world and make judgments. I have a chapter in part one where I sketch out the significant changes in worldview in the modern era.

In the modern astrology section I include critiques of the assumptions that our modern world makes when we look out at the cosmos, assumptions that are invisible to us since they are the water we swim in. The purpose of the critiques of the modern astrologers is to bring to awareness and make explicit the assumptions they make about the world, and the implications of those assumptions. I examine the actual words the astrologers wrote, and interpret them in their normal meanings. I also highlight the strengths and significant contributions that modern astrology makes, as I think we can benefit by combining the strengths of both modern and traditional astrology, and use each one's strengths to balance and complement the other's weak points.

Part Two: The Eternal Law. This section is the core and pivot of the entire book. For the traditional meaning of Saturn to make sense you need to have a supporting worldview, a way of thinking, that supports its meaning. The purpose of the second section is to provide that context and support.

The traditional meanings of Saturn are based on the assumption that there is an eternal order and pattern to the cosmos - not something

Introduction

that we humans have created and projected out from our minds, but an order that is part of the cosmos itself, both within our minds and in the underlying structure of the universe as a whole. Saturn's full meaning includes an eternal moral law integrated into the underlying structure of the cosmos.

In this section I look back to the fundamentals of the Platonic tradition to argue that there is such an eternal order, and that it is still alive and meaningful in our modern world. In our modern world there are still very good living reasons for thinking in terms of an eternal law in both the scientific sense and the moral and ethical sense.

So, while Part One is the historical survey, Part Two provides the frame of reference for the traditional meanings of Saturn to still make sense by laying out the philosophical and ethical underpinnings of Saturn's meaning.

Part Three: Essays on Saturn Themes. In the third section are essays on Saturn related themes that I think need to be revisited in the context of our modern popular culture. I am concentrating on the difficult or negative aspects of Saturn and human existence that we would just as soon not have to deal with in our modern world. This is in contrast to the common modern approach to heavily emphasize viewing Saturn, and everything else in astrology, in a positive light. I embrace these difficult dimensions of Saturn - suffering, aging, death, the problem of human evil - and argue that they are part of the full human experience, and that our lives are richer when we acknowledge and embrace them.

Note: Those of you who are familiar with my online blog may have seen articles which I wrote on the topic of Saturn's symbolism being feminine. Those essays are not included in this book. That topic will be addressed in a separate book in the future.

The Chesterton Test

At various points in this book I will be referring to what I call the Chesterton Test. I name it after the great British journalist and writer G K Chesterton. This quote is from his book with the very unfashionable title, *Orthodoxy*.

> Long words go rattling by us like long railway trains. We know they are carrying thousands who are too tired or too indolent to walk and think for themselves.
>
> It is a good exercise to try for once in a way to express any opinion one holds in words of one syllable.
>
> If you say "The social utility of the indeterminate sentence is recognized by all criminologists as a part of our sociological evolution towards a more humane and scientific view of punishment," you can go on talking like that for hours with hardly a movement of the gray matter inside your skull.
>
> But if you begin "I wish Jones to go to gaol and Brown to say when Jones shall come out," you will discover, with a thrill of horror, that you are obliged to think.
>
> The long words are not the hard words; it is the short words that are hard.

I will apply the Chesterton Test to quotes from some of the astrologers we review. The purpose is to help us think clearly about what is being said, and help us understand the implications. The sort of thinking that goes with Saturn has to do with simplicity and clarity, stripping away excess fluff and noise to let the clear meaning be visible.

Hopefully this book will be both short, and hard.

Part One: Historical Survey

We are going to start with a survey of the meanings attributed to Saturn throughout the history of Western astrology. There are some interesting patterns here. If we start with Vettius Valens, one of the earliest Hellenistic era astrologers, and go right through the Persian and Arabic periods, into Bonatti's compilation and the landmark English work, William Lilly's *Christian Astrology*, we will that there is a remarkable consistency of meaning throughout this entire era. We are recognizably looking at a single tradition spanning from the second to the seventeenth century.

As we get closer to our modern era there are some major shifts. Looking at quotes from two astrologers from the nineteenth century, we can begin to see a shift of emphasis. Once we hit the twentieth century and the birth of modern astrology the meanings of Saturn shift quite dramatically. We are still recognizably dealing with the same planet, but the style is different, the emphases are very different, and some old meanings are lost. This shift, from traditional to modern astrology, also involves a very different view of the world. I devote a chapter here to comparing traditional and modern worldviews to give a feel for that change.

In the remainder of this section I examine a series of modern astrologers, from early twentieth century up to today, including popular and influential astrologers like Liz Greene and Steven Forrest. In this section I am doing some critiquing of the descriptions, and the purpose of that critique is to bring to light the kinds of modern assumptions we make that color their interpretation. We are modern fish swimming in a different kind of water, and in this section I am trying to make the water visible. I then conclude with a chapter on the unique contributions of modern astrology. There are some important developments in the twentieth century that enrich our practice of astrology, and I want to recognize them.

Vettius Valens, Anthology

Vettius Valens of Antioch (c. 120- 175 AD) is the author of the *Anthology*, the earliest working astrologer's handbook we have, the record of how a working astrologer describes Saturn. It is one of the books at the center of a contemporary revival of interest in Hellenistic astrology.

This first series of quotes are from a section on the meanings of each of the seven planets in turn.

> Saturn makes those born under him petty, malignant, careworn, self-depreciating, solitary, deceitful, secretive in their trickery, strict, downcast, with a hypocritical air, squalid, black-clad, importunate, sad-looking, miserable, with a nautical bent, plying waterside trades.

Note the connection with water, and also with traits that make a person small, or negative, or limited, or untrustworthy. Self-depreciating here means limiting or cutting down oneself. Also note the connection with the color black, and with bad fortune. Another cluster of meanings relates to deceiving, hiding, tricking or being hypocritical. If you think of being in the light as honest, then being in the darkness of Saturn is deceiving, hiding, dishonest.

> Saturn also causes humblings, sluggishness, unemployment, obstacles in business, interminable lawsuits, subversion of business, secrets, imprisonment, chains, griefs, accusations, tears, bereavement, capture, exposures of children.

This section includes problems, bad fortunes, death and events that block or limit. There are connections with things that take a long time or stretch on, and connections with secrecy, things that are hidden or in the dark.

Vettius Valens, Anthology

> Saturn makes serfs and farmers because of its rule over the land, and it causes men to be renters of property, tax farmers, and violent in action.

Here we see the connection of Saturn with land, with what is hard and physical. This includes people who work with the land, as renters, as servants or as owner.

> It puts into one's hands great ranks and distinguished positions, supervisions, management of others' property, and the fathership of others' children.

Saturn is associated with power and authority over others. This relates to Saturn being the outermost planet, above all the others. Associated with this we see themes of rulership, management, and law. Saturn is also related to age as part of authority.

> Of materials, it rules lead, wood, and stone.

> Of the limbs of the body, it rules the legs, the knees, the tendons, the lymph, the phlegm, the bladder, the kidneys, and the internal, hidden organs.

> Things hard or things hidden. Of Saturn's Signs, Capricorn rules knees, Aquarius rules the shins and ankles, Libra rules the kidneys.

> Saturn is indicative of injuries arising from cold and moisture, such as dropsy, neuralgia, gout, cough, dysentery, hernia, spasms.

Again we see the early connection of Saturn with cold and wet. In later quotes we will see Saturn associated with diseases related to the body drying up or becoming inflexible, like arthritis. The cold and dry associations with become more dominant as we move through time. The cold/dry association relates to the system of humors where Saturn is classified as melancholic, the most cold and dry of the planets. Where planets are associated with a system of classification, the meanings that don't fit within the classification tend to fall away.

> It is indicative of these syndromes: possession, homosexuality, and depravity.

These are associations of Saturn with things evil, or corrupt, sinful or deviant.

> Saturn makes bachelors and widows, bereavements, and childlessness.

This connects Saturn with losses by death, or from an inability to give birth.

> It causes violent deaths by water, strangulation, imprisonment, or dysentery.

All of these Saturn associations are bad fortune related to death, and again the association with water.

> It also causes falling on the face. It is the star of Nemesis; it is of the day sect.

Nemesis is the Greek goddess of vengeance or retributive justice, a punishment that is deserved, though one that could be delayed. This highlights a connection of Saturn with justice, judgment, the punitive side of the law. Earlier we saw an association of Saturn with law as related to authority.

> It is like castor in color and astringent in taste.

Astringent tastes make the mouth shrivel or shrink or dry up, so it is related to Saturn being cold and dry.

This next series gives quotes is from a later section where Valens gives the meanings of Saturn paired with each of the other planets.

> When **Saturn and Jupiter** are together, they are in agreement with each other, and they bring about benefits from legacies and adoptions, and they cause men to be

> masters of property consisting of land, to be guardians, managers of others' property, stewards, and tax gatherers.

These meanings are almost all positive, and combine authority and control. Legacies are inheritances that come from deaths. We also have the connection again of Saturn with land, so controlling the wealth of land.

> **Saturn and Mars** are hostile, productive of reversals and ruin. They bring family quarrels, disharmony, and hatred, along with treachery, plots, malevolence, and trials. However, if these stars are not in their own or in operative signs, and if they have benefics in aspect, they produce distinguished and noble nativities, although unsteady in their happiness and prone to unexpected dangers and treachery.

The two malefics together are violent and destructive. The references to nobility refers to the power that these malefics could exert if in a prominent position. Whether powerful or not there is an instability and lack of trustworthiness to the action of these two planets combined. You would not want to be on the bad side of a person with these traits.

> **Saturn and Mercury** are allies and productive of activities/employment. They do, however, bring slanders about religion, lawsuits, and debts, as well as disturbances about written matters and money. On the other hand, these stars make men who are not without resources and not unintelligent, with much experience and awareness, and who are curious, far-seeing scholars, seekers after mystic lore, revering the gods, but with much on their consciences.

Combining Saturn with Mercury's rulership of commerce and we get control of money. Mercury is also associated with learning, which combines with Saturn to give depth, profundity, a mystic side, a researcher into hidden truths. Overall Saturn and Mercury together is seen as a positive combination.

> **Saturn and Venus** act harmoniously with respect to activities/employment: they promote success with respect to entanglements and marriage, agreeing and beneficial only for a time, not to the end. Indeed they cause abuse, divorces, inconstancy, and death, often entangling men with the base-born and the lowly, and causing them to fall into harm and lawsuits.

Most of these relate to Venus as associated with relationships and marriage. The Saturn Venus connection is good when it is stable, but filled with problems and strife when debilitated. You also have the connection of Saturn with death.

> **Saturn and the Moon** are beneficial, productive of money, estates, ship ownership, and profits from the deceased, especially if the moon happens to be in the part of its orbit just following first visibility and has benefics in aspect. Then it causes association with the great, gifts, and the discomfiture of enemies. This combination, however, is unsteady with respect to possession, and with respect to women it is insecure and painful because of separations, hatred, and grief. It also produces bodily suffering, sudden fits, pains of the governing faculties and nerves, as well as the deaths of important figures.

This is the Moon ruling changing fortunes, and again we see the connection of Saturn with death, the deceased, and legacies. The Moon is also related to women and thus to separations. The Moon relates to bodily health, which combined with Saturn gives physical suffering.

> **Saturn and the Sun** are at odds, giving and taking away possessions and friendships maliciously. Therefore those born under such a juncture suffer secret enmities and threats from great persons and are plotted against by some and live hated to the end. Playing their part well, they

outlive most of their enemies. They are, however, not without resources, but are disturbed and long-suffering. They are self-controlled in this onslaught of reversals.

Most of these Saturn-Sun meanings come from the fact that the two planets are in opposition in the Zodiac signs they rule, Saturn in Aquarius opposite Sun in Leo. We have the hottest and brightest planet opposite the coldest and darkest. Saturn stands for the opposition aspect in general, and thus anything that blocks or hinders.

Firmicus Maternus, Mathesis

Julius Firmicus Maternus (c. 285-360) was a Roman lawyer, astrologer and writer. His book *Mathesis* is the longest and most extensive astrology treatise that we have from this early classical era. Firmicus places a very strong importance on sect, whether a chart is diurnal or nocturnal, day or night. Saturn is considered a day planet, so the meanings for Saturn in a day chart are much more positive than for a night chart.

I include excerpts here from the meanings attributed to Saturn in a sample of the houses. You will see that they pick up on the same themes that are mentioned in other traditional texts and applies them to the house context, making them more positive or negative depending on the sect of the chart.

> Saturn posited in the 4th house, will if it holds this house by day, make those greedy for money, and custodians of gold and silver. But if it was in this sign by night, it dissipates the paternal inheritance, and will cause the quick death of the father.

Here Saturn is associated with the father, with age, and with wealth.

> Saturn posited in the 9th house from the ASC will make famous mages or renowned philosophers, or priests of temples, always famous in their reputation for magic. According to the quality of the sign, it also makes diviners, prophets and astrologers always industrious for their true interpretation, and whose responses are such as if they were brought forth by a kind of divine authority.

Saturn is associated with wisdom and profundity, things that are deep, so this also relates to exploring hidden and deep and occult matters. Depth of thought and hidden matters are Saturn themes since the earliest texts, and the association here with the ninth house of religion brings those out.

Firmicus Maternus, Mathesis

> But if Saturn is posited in this house by night, it will make the native to suffer from the wrath of the Gods, and the displeasure of Emperors.

Here we have negative judgments from those in authority, whether Gods or Emperors. Saturn is either working with the gods or judged in wrath by the gods. Notice that it does not say anything about the person influenced by Saturn doing the judging, but rather suffering the judgment.

> Saturn posited in the tenth house from the ASC will make Emperors, military commanders, prefects of the Imperial Bodyguard. If, with Saturn posited thus in those places in which it is exalted, in the MC by day, it will make honest farmers with honest customs, but wealthy ones, and those whose possessions are always adjacent to the sea or rivers or to swamps. It will also give the greatest assets, great glory, and inheritances from greater persons.

Here Saturn is associated with positions of authority and control, or their exact opposite, depending on its condition. As the outermost planet, when Saturn is associated with control it is rulership from the top, a position of extreme power. At the opposite extreme it can be the bottom, slaves and serfs, those subjected to harsh control. We also see the persistent connection of Saturn with land and water together.

> But if it was found by night in the MC, it denotes misfortunes. It will cause the loss of his inheritance, it will deny marriage, it will deny children...But in particular, the star of Saturn posited by night in any angle denotes the greatest evils for the nativity, for it kills the wives, ruins the children, and always indicates the bitter pains of bereavement.

Saturn is a day planet, so Saturn at night is at its worst and is associated with death, loss and bad fortune.

Abu Ma'shar, The Great Introduction

Abu Ma'shar (c. 787-886) was an Arab astrologer and astronomer and a very prolific writer, and many of his books have come down to us, either in Latin or in the original Arabic. The following text is from his *Great Introduction* and is included in *Introductions to Traditional Astrology* by Ben Dykes, along with quotes from other important Arabic astrologers that are along the same lines.

This text appears in the book by Ben Dykes as a single long paragraph. I have broken it up into smaller pieces since it is not really a continuous train of thought, but rather a collection of attributes.

> Therefore, the nature of Saturn is cold, dry, melancholic, dark, of heavy harshness. And perhaps he will be cold and moist, heavy, of stinking odor, and he is of much eating and true esteem.

Here we have the primary association of Saturn with dark and cold. Sometimes Saturn is cold and dry, sometimes cold and moist. Here the connection of Saturn with melancholy and cold-dry is emphasized first. Saturn is stinking as in something unpleasant or poisonous or rotting. Things which are rotting or decay are in the process of dying. We also see an association with true esteem, an earned or deserved respect. This is the only place I have seen Saturn associated with much eating.

> And he signifies works of moisture and the cultivation of land, and peasants, and village companions, and the settlement of lands, also buildings and waters and rivers, and the quantities or measures of things, and the divisions of the earth, also affluence and a multitude of assets, and masteries which are done by hand, greed and the greatest poverty and the poor.

Saturn relates to earth, and people who work the earth, and earth near water, so again we see the connection with moisture. The connection with measuring associates with limiting, dividing, delimiting or setting boundaries or frameworks.

Saturn also is connected to extremes related to wealth - affluence from controlling much, or poverty from being lowly, cast down. There is an association with greed as a moral corruption, and greed as wanting to clutch and control more than one's fair share.

> And he signifies travel by sea, and foreign travel that is far away and of great length, and bad. And cleverness, envy and wits and seductions, and boldness in dangers and impediment, and hesitation, and being singular, and a scarcity of association with men, and pride and magnanimity and bluffing and bragging and the subjection of men, also the managers of a kingdom and of every work which comes to be with force and with evil and injuries and a tendency to anger, even warriors and fettering and prison,

Here we see more connections with Saturn as clever, wise, crafty, action that is not overt and blunt but covert, in the darkness, hidden.

> also truth in words, and esteem, and prudence and understanding, and experience and offense, and obstinacy and a multitude of thoughts and depth of counsel, and insistence, and stubbornness in his method.

These are positive traits from age, perseverance and experience. We have the wisdom that comes with age. This is Saturn as profundity, deep rather than shallow. Saturn is deep in multiple senses of the term. Saturn when reliable is truth, Saturn when unreliable is falsehood, craftiness and deception.

> He does not easily get angry, and if he were angry he would not be able to make up his own mind.

> He wishes good to no one.

This is Saturn as a malefic, wishing harm on others.

Abu Ma'shar, The Great Introduction

> And he signifies old men and weighty men and burdens and fear, griefs and sorrow and complication of the mind.

Age and sorrow are common Saturn themes.

> And fraud and affliction and difficulty and loss;

Again we have Saturn as malefic, and again the association with fraud, lying, hiding.

> also ancestors and what is left behind by the dead, mourning, and being orphaned, and old things. Even grandfathers and fathers and brothers, and senior people and slaves and mule drivers and men who are blamed, and robbers and those who dig up graves and who rob the garments of the dead.

These are associations with age, or male relatives. We also see lowly trades, or loss of freedom, trades associated with death, and digging into the earth.

> And he signifies a great length of thought and a scarcity of speaking and the knowledge of secrets, and one does not know what is in his mind, nor does a wise person make disclosures to him about every obscure matter. And he signifies austerity and the ascetics of religions.

Here the we have he association with profundity of thought, which comes from work over a sustained time. We also have Saturn as hidden, taciturn, withdrawn, quiet, secretive. Saturnian religious traits are severe, self-limiting, and monastic.

Al-Biruni

Al-Biruni (c.973-1048) was an Arab scholar, scientist and author. These quotes are taken from his *Book of Instruction in the Elements of the Art of Astrology*. This book covers the planets in a series of sections according to the subject areas. I am here drawing together the data on Saturn from several of the topic areas. The bracketed text gives the section titles. As with other traditional sources there are brief lists of associations that are very rich and complex. These aren't streamlined keywords as in modern astrology, they are qualities that have an open-ended metaphoric quality, and they are also rooted in qualities of physically existing things.

> [NATURES OF THE PLANETS AND THEIR INDICATORS] Saturn is extremely cold and dry. The greater malefic. Male. Diurnal. Disagreeable and astringent, offensively acid, stinking, jet-black also black mixed with yellow, lead colour, pitch-dark.
>
> Saturn: Coldest, hardest, most stinking and most powerful of things. Shortness, dryness, hardness, heaviness. Barren mountains.

These associations are mainly from the cold dry humors, and associations with darkness and rotting.

> [BUILDINGS AND COUNTRIES] Saturn: Underground canals and vaults, wells, old buildings, desolate roads, lairs of wild beasts, deserts full of them, stables for horses, asses, and camels, and elephant's houses.

Saturn goes with dark places, isolated places, lowly animals or animals that are beasts carrying heavy burdens.

> [RELATIONS AND CONNECTIONS, FIGURE, AND FACE] Saturn: Fathers, grandfathers, older brothers and slaves. Ugly, tall, wizened, sour face, large head, eyebrows

joined, small eyes, wide mouth, thick lips, downcast look, much black hair, short neck, coarse hand, short fingers, awkward figure, legs crooked, big feet.

[DISPOSITION AND MANNERS] Saturn: Fearful, timid, anxious, suspicious, miserly, a malevolent plotter, sullen and proud, melancholy, truth-telling, grave, trusty, unwilling to believe good of anyone, engrossed in his own affairs and consequently indicates discord, and either ignorance or intelligence, but the ignorance is concealed.

Saturn here is isolated, and again we see the association with things hidden, indirect, in the darkness, not open and honest, hence also suspicious, selfish.

[ACTIVITIES, INSTINCTS AND MORALS] Saturn: Exile and poverty, or wealth acquired by his own trickery and that of others, failure in business, vehemence, confusion, seeking solitariness, enslaving people by violence or treachery, fraud, weeping and wailing and lamentation.

The ways listed here that Saturn gains wealth and control are negative - deception, violence, treachery.

[RELIGIONS, PICTURES OF PLANETS] Saturn: Jews and those who dress in black. Old man seated on a wolf, in his right hand the head of a man and in the left a man's hand; or according to another picture, mounted on a bright bay horse, on his head a helmet, in the left hand a shield and in the right a sword.

Planets were associated with religions, and Saturn was associated with the Jews as the people of the Torah, the Law, just as Saturn is associated with law in general. This also relates to Judaism as being a very old religion, a fore-runner or ancestor of Christianity which was associated with Jupiter, the next planet down. Saturn is the planet of Law as Jupiter is the planet of Mercy.

[TRADES, PROFESSIONS] Saturn: Building, paymaster, farming, reclaiming land and distribution of water, apportioning money and heritages, grave-digging; selling things made of iron, lead, bone, hair, copper, black slaves; knowledge used for bad purposes, such acts of government as lead to evil oppression, wrath, captivity, torture.

Here are associations with land, or again land and water together, with death, and with lowly people. Again we see the connection with corrupt motives; Saturn is a corrupt or oppressive or evil ruler who causes pain and malice.

Avraham Ibn-Ezra, The Beginning of Wisdom

Avraham Ibn-Ezra ben Meir (c 1089-1164) was born in Spain in the middle ages and moved to Israel in the latter part of his life. Ibn-Ezra was Jewish and his writings are in Hebrew. The astrology writings of Ibn-Ezra are in the same general tradition as the Arabic astrologers, which all have their roots in the original Greek tradition.

> Saturn is cold and dry and his nature is evil and harmful. He indicates destruction, and ruin, and death, and grief, and mourning and weeping and crying, and ancient things.

> His share of the human spirit is the power of thought.

Note the recurring theme of Saturn as thought, as depth, as wisdom, as profundity. I think this is related to the relation of Saturn and Mercury that Valens talked about, with both having connections with thought. This also relates to the connection of Saturn and the Law.

> ...in general all old people, and farmers, and builders, and tanners, and those who clean lavatories, slaves, the inferior, robbers, ditch and grave diggers, and undertakers. In his share of places of the earth are the caves and wells, and pits, and prisons, and every dark and uninhabited place, and the cemeteries.

Saturn is connected with old age, with people who work with earth, lowly trades in general, and trades connected to death. We also see places connected to death, or confinement, or underground, or hidden, or dark.

> His nature is cold and dry, and his flavor is the astringent and everything that has disagreeable taste and smell.

This is Saturn as cold and dry rather than cold and wet. The cold and wet qualities of Saturn seem to be emphasized less in later texts, probably because of the systematizing of the four humors or temperaments. Associations that did not fit in with the humors tend to be emphasized less or to be dropped.

> In his share of the human nature is the contemplation, little talk, astuteness, isolation from people, controlling them and winning and levying taxes, and getting angry, keeping one's word, deep thought, knowledge of secrets and the worship of God, inferior people, contrariness, fear, worry, coveting, and in general habitually lying with little usefulness and much ruin.

Again we see the mix of contradictory attributions - profundity, quietness, hidden knowledge or worship, but also deceit, lying, hiding the truth. Both themes are associated with Saturn from the earliest texts.

> Saturn indicates tilling the land, building, mining metals, seeking hidden treasures, digging and examining things of the dead, and everything that lasts for many years.

This is Saturn associated with earth, with long duration, and the dead.

> He indicates fathers and grandfathers, the deceased, crying and separation, wandering, poverty, humiliation, distant bad roads where danger lurks and he has no success in all undertaking.

Saturn as an old and slow moving planet is associated with fathers and grandfathers. The other attributions are related to bad fortune that puts one in lowly conditions.

Bonatti, Book of Astronomy

Guido Bonatti (1210-1296) was a medieval Italian astrologer. His magnum opus written in Latin is *The Book of Introduction to the Judgments of the Stars*, better known as *The Book of Astronomy*. It is a massive compendium of material from the great astrologers of the Arabic tradition, and is likely the single most influential collection transmitting much of that tradition to later astrologers in Europe and the Western world.

> Saturn is a masculine, diurnal planet, and he works at intemperate coldness and dryness. And he is a significator of fathers and grandfathers and all ancestors.

In the system of humors Saturn is intemperate or excessive cold and dry. Cold and wet significations have mostly been dropped.

> ... for he naturally signifies the person or body of the native, on account of the fact that the first thing which happens to a man is the physical person through which being is given to him.

Saturn relates to the body as a boundary or limit or container or structure. It also relates to body as being physical, of the earth.

> And Saturn is in the first circle of the planets, and is the first planet in their order, and whom all others follow, and is even the first one who exercises his operation in a conceived child after the falling of the seed into the womb, by binding and uniting together the matter from which the conceived child is formed.

There is an association here of Saturn with the first and eighth houses, the houses of birth and death. We see Saturn associated with the physical, at the borderline of the physical mutable world, hence the giver of form to things of matter and time. The nine months of gestation were given to the seven Chaldean planets in order, starting with Saturn in month one, Jupiter in month two and so on, then around to Saturn again month eight. The houses were associated with the planets in the same order, with house one Saturn, house two Jupiter, and on to house seven with the Moon, then the order repeats with house eight Saturn and so on. As the outermost planet Saturn is the first planet we pass as we descend and enter the world, and the last we pass as we exit the world at death. It is connected with beginnings and endings, and with borders.

> Saturn is a significator of fathers, and of old things, and the burdensome things they have in light of his slow and burdened motion, and his heaviness; and therefore they made him the significator of older parents and of ancient things and burdensome things.
>
> And Saturn is everything which signifies the severity of intemperate cold and dryness. And of the humors hie signifies melancholy... and with slowness and heaviness of limbs of the native's body.

Coldness and dryness together tend to shrink things, and this is related to severity, and to problems from age, heaviness, and depression.

> And if he were of good condition, it signifies profoundness of knowledge, and good and deep counsel, such that another will hardly or never know how to improve on it.

Again we see Saturn connected to profound knowledge, depth, wisdom, good counsel.

> And of professions he signifies ancient things and those full of labor, and aquatic works or those which take place near water (like mills, bridges, ships and the like), and the bringing forth of waters, and the cultivation of the earth (like fields, planting trees, the building of houses - and especially of the houses of religious men wearing black clothing - if he were made fortunate and of good condition.

Here we have the connection of land, and land near water, and also work with the land. There are connections with religion and the color black, hence monks, who would also be severe and renunciate.

> If however he were made unfortunate and of bad condition, he signifies old and low class things, like working with hoes, the digging of base pits, and in stinking places, and the carrying of stones and cement to walls by the neck, and especially to underground walls, or those of cities, and which are next to pits, and the making of many things which come to be of brick, and the like. And often such people live in labor and distress and poverty, and they eat bad and stinking foods.

This is Saturn as low in several senses - dark, poor, bad condition, physically low and unhealthy places, and low income or poverty, also low quality foods, foods that are rotting and dying.

> And if he were in good condition, he signifies great and wealthy sailors, and he will be of true esteem, and ample and patient or enduring.

This is a place where we still see the association with water, but also sometimes wealth that comes from ventures over water or from real estate.

> And if he were of bad condition, the native will be undistinguished, sad, grieving, of bad suspicion, eager to suspect every evil, and in rousing men by whispers and evil incitements.

This group of associations is complex - things low and poor quality, but also a secretive, suspicious and cynical quality - hidden, so whispers and slanders, words spoken out of the view of the light. This is Saturn as malefic, rejoicing in inciting evil. Saturn is corrupt as in rotting but also corrupt as in impure or corrupt motives.

And if he were of good condition, he signifies old and durable things, as are inheritances which come from any source (and especially from the dead), and estates which are acquired by him by lawful means more so than by wicked means.

Saturn is connected to inheritances, money from death. There is the association with ancestors, the aged and dead, those who have gone before, the past. Saturn also relates to age in the sense of durable, things that last for a long time.

William Lilly: Christian Astrology

William Lilly (1602-1681) is the most famous of all English astrologers, and his classic textbook, *Christian Astrology*, is arguably the greatest and most influential astrology text in the English language. The text of this section is from book One covering the basic elements of astrology. Since this book is so very influential I will quote and comment on it extensively. The section headings I use here show up in the margins of the original printed edition.

> **Names** - He is called usually Saturn, but in some Authors Chronos, Phoenon, Falcifer.

Chronus or Kronos are Greek names associated with Saturn. The name Saturn is Roman rather than Greek. Chronus or Kronus is Saturn, husband of Rhea, and Chronos is a god associated with time. They are originally two different gods and concepts, and the two have been combined into one over time, and both are now associated with Saturn. Phoenon is another Greek name for Saturn, and I was unable to find any other meaning. The only reference I could find to Falcifer is a name meaning 'Lord of Darkness', a fallen angel or demon. Lilly lists these traditional names of Saturn, but does not refer to or develop the mythology. None of the meaning or interpretation is tied to these names. The heavy emphasis on mythological interpretation is a modern development.

> **Color** - He is the supremest or highest of all Planets; is placed betwixt Jupiter and the Firmament, he is not very bright or glorious, nor doth he twinkle or sparkle, but is of a Pale, Wan or Leaden, Ashy colour slow in motion.

Pale, leaden, ashy, grey, slow, are all typical Saturn qualities. By supremest he means furthest from the Sun of the moving planets. The Firmament is the unchanging sphere of the fixed stars, which was considered to be fixed, immutable, unchanging. Note that Saturn is the planet at the border of moving and unmoving, temporal and eternal, changing and unchanging.

Recall the association of Saturn with Lord of Darkness. Saturn is at the outer ring between eternal and temporal, heaven and earth, the guardian of this fallen, dark, mutable world.

> **Motion** - Finishing his Course through the twelve signs of the Zodiac in 29 years, 157 days, or thereabouts; his middle motion is two minutes and one second; his diurnal motion sometimes is three, four, five, or six minutes, or seldom more.

Saturn is the slowest moving of the traditional planets. Slowness, and long periods of time, are both associated with Saturn.

> **Latitude** - His greatest North Latitude from the Ecliptic is two degrees 48 minutes; his South Latitude from the Ecliptic is two degrees 49 minutes; and more than this he hath not.

> **Houses** - In the Zodiac he hath two of the twelve Signs for his Houses, viz. Capricorn his Night house, Aquarius his Day house; he has his Exaltation in Libra, he receives his Fall in Aries; he rejoiceth in the sign Aquarius.

The two signs ruled by Saturn, Capricorn and Aquarius, are the two that are furthest from the two Lights, Sun and Moon. As the Lights rule summer signs, Saturn rules the two signs of the dead of winter, the time of extreme cold and darkness.

> **Triplicity** - He governeth the Airy Triplicity by day, which is composed of these Signs; Gemini, Libra, Aquarius.

> He continueth Retrograde 140 dayes. He is five days in his first station before Retrogradation, and so many in his second station before Direction.

> **Nature** - He is a Diurnal Planet, Cold and Dry (being far removed from the heat of the Sun) and moist Vapours, Melancholic, Earthly, Masculine, the greater Infortune, author of Solitariness, Malevolent, &c.

Saturn is described both as cold and dry, and as cold and moist. The common thread is extreme cold, that makes things wither. Isolated cold places do tend to get damp, as the air can't hold very much moisture so it condenses out. The places are dark, unpleasant, solitary, isolated, stagnant, unhealthy. Think of the cold of the dead of winter at night, or the cold of a dark and unheated basement.

When we consider Saturn as a diurnal or day planet, it is worth noting that the other day planets, Sun, Jupiter and sometimes Mercury, are warm. Saturn is extreme cold, dark and dry, so it is grouped with the day planets in order to moderate those properties. The other malefic, hot and dry Mars, is grouped with the cool night planets to moderate that extreme heat.

> **Manners & Actions, when well dignified** - Then he is profound in Imagination, in his Acts severe, in words reserved, in speaking and giving very spare, in labour patient, in arguing or disputing grave, in obtaining the goods of this life studious and solicitous, in all manner of actions austere.

These are the virtues of age and experience, and the wisdom that comes with that. They are related to patience, slowness and depth.

> **When ill dignified** - Then he is envious, covetous, jealous and mistrustful, timorous, sordid, outwardly dissembling, sluggish, suspicious, stubborn, a contemner of women, a close liar, malicious, murmuring, never contented, ever repining.

These are the sort of vices that come from becoming shriveled and dried up inside. They are shrinking, defensive, covert, furtive, dishonest, sneaky. These are the vices of hiding in darkness. Think of people hiding behind the anonymity of black masks and in a group, threatening and attacking.

> **Corporature** - Most part his Body more cold and dry, of a middle stature; his complexion pale, swarthish or muddy,

his Eyes little and black, looking downward, a broad Forehead, black or sad Hair, and it hard or rugged, great Ears; hanging, lowring Eyebrows, thick Lips and Nose, a rare or thin Beard, a lumpish, unpleasant Countenance, either holding his Head forward or stooping, his Shoulders broad and large, and many times crooked, his Belly somewhat short and lank, his Thighs spare; lean and not long; his Knees and Feet indecent, many times shoveling or hitting one against another, &c.

This is Saturn associated with being ill-proportioned, crude, misshapen, ugly.

Saturn Oriental - You must observe, if Saturn be Oriental of the Sun, the stature is more short, but decent and well composed.

Occidental - The man is more black and lean, and fewer Hairs; and again, if he want latitude, the body is more lean, if he have great latitude, the body is more fat or fleshy; if the latitude be Meridional or South, more fleshy; if the latitude be Meridional or South, more fleshy, but quick in motion. If the latitude be North, hairy and much flesh.

Saturn in his first station, a little fat. In his second station, fat, ill favoured Bodies, and weak; and this observe constantly in all the other Planets.

Quality of Men - In generall he signifieth Husbandmen, Clowns, Beggars, Day labourers, Old-men, Fathers, Grandfathers, Monks, Jesuits, Sectarists.

A planet is considered oriental when it rises before the Sun, and occidental when it rises after. The word clown here means awkward, ill-bred, crude, oafish, lower class, and the list includes lower class groups getting little respect. We also have associations with age and seriousness. The religious associations are severe, isolated, penitential, and associated with the color black. A Sectarist is a person of a severe and prejudiced group, related to heretic, outside of the mainstream, that looks askance on others.

> **Profession** - Curriers, Night-farmers, Miners under ground, Tinners, Potters, Broom men, Plumbers, Brickmakers, Malsters, Chimney sweepers, Sextons of Churches, Bearers of dead corpses, Scavengers, Hostlers, Colliers, Carters, Gardeners, Ditchers, Chandlers, Diers of Black cloth, an Herdsman, Shepherd or Cow-keeper.

A Currier works with tanning hides. A Malster is a maker of malt - ie, a brewer. A Hostler is a groom or stable worker. A Collier is a coal miner. A Carter is someone who pushes small carts, or hauls away garbage. Most of these professions are lower class, low paying, and many are unskilled manual labor. Some are associated with dirt, or decay, or death, or night, or underground. Some are done in isolation, away from other people, like herdsmen and shepherds. Regarding the association with things underground, Hell is traditionally below the earth - the Latin word for Hell, Infernum, basically means inferior or underground or below.

> **Sicknesses** - All Impediments in the right Ears, Teeth, all quartan Agues proceeding of cold, dry and melancholy Distempers, Leprosies, Rheumes, Consumptions, black Jaundies, Palsies, Tremblings, vain Fears, Fantasies, Dropsy, the Hand and Footgout, Apoplexies, Dog-hunger, too much flux of the Hemoroids, Ruptures if in Scorpio or Leo, in any ill aspect with Venus.

Quartan ague is a disease like influenza that has a fever, sweating and convulsions, called Quartan for a fever that recurred every 4 days. Think of the sort of diseases you would get hanging out in a cold wet basement. These are diseases that waste or decay the body, where it starts to rot while it is still alive. Vain fears and fantasies are like a rotting of the imagination, opening up to unhealthy and demonic forces. There is a very common Catholic night hour hymn that prays to be protected from nightly fears and fantasies and from false and polluting dreams, dreams sent by the devil to ensnare people. That is the sort of thing we are looking at here.

>**Savors** - Sour, Bitter, Sharp, in mans body he principally ruleth the Spleen.

>**Herbs** - He governeth Beirsfoot, Starwort, Wolfbane, Hemlock, Ferne, Hellebor the white and black, Henbane, Ceterach or Fingerferne, Clotbur or Burdock, Parsnip, Dragon, Pulse, Vervine, Mandrake, Poppy, Mosse, Nightshade, Bythwind, Angelica, Sage, Box, Tutfan, Orage or golden Hearb, Spinach, Shepherds Purse, Cumin, Horitaile, Fumitory.

There are a couple of common themes here. Many of these plants are deadly poisons. Some of them grow in dark or shady or mossy places. Others are noted from having a sharp or bitter or unpleasant taste.

>**Plants and Trees** - Tamarisk, Savine, Sene, Capers, Rue or Hearbgrice, Polipody, Willow or Sallow Tree, Yew-tree, Cypress tree, Hemp, Pine-tree.

>**Beasts etc.** - The Ass, Cat Hare, Mouse, Mole, Elephant, Bear, Dog, Wolf, Basilisk, Crocodile, Scorpion, Toad, Serpent, Adder, Hog, all manner of creeping Creatures breeding of putrification, either in the Earth, Water or Ruins of Houses.

These are creatures of the night; sneaky, furtive, hidden; venomous, dangerous; living in corrupt or decaying or unhealthy places.

>**Fishes, Birds etc.** - The Eel, Tortoise, Shellfishes. The Bat or Blood-black, Crow, Lapwing, Owl, Gnat, Crane, Peacock, Grasshopper, Thrush, Blackbird, Ostrich, Cuckoo.

>**Places** - He delights in Deserts, Woods, obscure Valleys, Caves, Dens, Holes, Mountains, or where men have been buried, Churchyards, &c. Ruinous Buildings, Coal mines,

> Sinks, Dirty or Stinking Muddy Places, Wells and Houses of Offices, &c.

We're seeing the same sorts of themes here, places that are hidden, or isolated, or underground, places associated with death or decay, unhealthy places.

> **Minerals** - He ruleth over Lead, the Leadstone, the Dross of all Metals, as also, the Dust and Rubbish of every thing.

Along with being a dull greyish black color, lead is also poisonous.

> **Stones** - Sapphire, Lapis Lazuli, all black, ugly Country Stones not polishable, and of a sad ashy or black color.

> **Weather** - He causeth Cloudy, Dark, obscure Air, cold and hurtful, thick, black and cadense Clouds: but of this more particularly in a Treatise by itself.

This describes air that is unhealthy in a Saturn sort of way - dark, thick, dense, cold.

> **Winds** - He delighteth in the East quarter of Heaven, and causeth Eastern Winds, at the time of gathering any Planet belonging to him, the Ancients did observe to turn their faces towards the East in his hour, and he, if possible, in an Angle, either in the Ascendant, or tenth, or eleventh house, the Moon applying by a Trine or Sextile to him.

> **Orb** - His Orb is nine degrees before and after; that is, his influence begins to work, when either he applies, or any Planet applies to him, and is within nine degrees of his aspect, and from that aspect.

> **Age** - As to Age, he relates to decrepit old men; Fathers, Grandfathers, the like in Plants, Trees, and all living Creatures.

His friends are Jupiter, Sun and Mercury, his enemies Mars and Venus. We call Saturday his day, for then he begins to rule at Sun rise, and ruleth the first hour and eighth of that day.

Saturn is a day planet, and Jupiter, Sun and sometimes Mercury are also day planets. Venus and Mars are two of the night planets. I would add the other night planet, the Moon, as an enemy of Saturn, or at least Saturn as the enemy of the Moon. Hard Saturn to Moon aspects are bad news for the Moon.

The Meanings of Saturn in Traditional Astrology

Now that we have surveyed several traditional authors you can see that there is a great deal of consistency of meaning across them. Here I want to draw out some of the common clusters of meaning, and look at where they may have come from.

As I have mentioned, I have a hunch that Saturn as cold and damp is an earlier attribution than cold and dry. In the system of the 4 humors Saturn is categorized as melancholic, cold and dry. This superseded the earlier association with water and damp.

A lot of the meanings of Saturn come from its opposition to the lights, primarily the Sun, but also the Moon. The cluster of meanings for Saturn come from its position in the Thema Mundi and the primary aspect of opposition in that diagram. There is a geometrical underpinning to the meanings of the planet. If we take a table of opposites and put the Sun in one column across from Saturn, we see several of the most important dimensions of Saturn's meaning.

Sun	Saturn
hot and dry	cold and damp
light	dark
day	night
summer	winter
revealed	concealed
high	low
height	depth

The Meanings of Saturn in Traditional Astrology

Both Sun and Moon are related to physical vitality, and Saturn is opposite both. Some meanings are from the opposition aspect itself - whatever blocks, delays, opposes.

Saturn's Place in the Traditional Cosmos

There are several other core principles that are derived from the physical characteristics of the planet and its location in the traditional cosmos. Some of the meanings come from Saturn being the planet furthest from the heat of the Sun, thus the extreme of cold and of dark. Saturn being the coldest, darkest and most distant planet is related to the opposition aspect and its place opposite the lights in Thema Mundi.

Saturn is a border planet at the edge of time and eternity, the unmoving and the moving. You have Saturn as borders, walls, structures, edges, containers, skin. Saturn on the edge of eternity also is the mediator of the eternal law and order of the heavens down into the mutable world. This is Saturn as judgment, related to the modern notion of karma, but also Saturn as wisdom meaning knowledge and understanding of those laws - combine law plus age and you get the wisdom of age. Saturn as the outermost planet is very much the planet of entire cycles, and the wisdom that comes from knowledge of the entire cycles.

As border or gateway between moving and unmoving, time and eternity, Saturn is death - and, as Bonatti pointed out, Saturn marks both the entry into time and the exit from time. This relates Saturn to the after death reckoning, the judgment where our lives are measured over against the eternal law. Saturn also comes to represent Time itself, the overall process, and thus also overall cycles, and the consequences of the passage of time.

Combine age plus cold plus damp and you get associations with decaying, rotting, unhealthy, diseased, dying. Some of the other

The Meanings of Saturn in Traditional Astrology

meanings come from Saturn being the slowest moving planet, hence associated with things that take a long time, move slowly, or are associated with age.

We can derive some main clusters of attributions of Saturn from various combinations of the basic meanings we have listed here.

Time - Many of the meanings come from Saturn's being on the border of eternity and time. Hence Saturn is associated with the passage of time. This has other related themes.

- Old age, which is the effect of time, and an age where you are very aware of time. In turn, Saturn is also associated with the elders, the aged, and with previous generations.

- The wisdom of old age, when you have the perspective on cycles that comes from time passage.

- Decaying, falling apart, as part of the passage of time; thus also corruption, decay, disease. Saturn seems to be especially related to diseases that are cold, or dry things up, or diseases that are like rotting or decay, so a skin disease like leprosy would be Saturnian.

- Saturn is thus also related to death, the inevitable consequence of life in time.

- Saturn is tradition, that which is passed down in time.

- Saturn relates to suffering, the effect of time, decay, delay etc. on people.

- Saturn and suffering can relate to moral law, and then you get suffering well, or enduring suffering for others.

Borders and Structures - This meaning also comes from being a border planet between time and timeless. Saturn is associated with containers like bodies, the skin of the body, the structure, the bones and teeth.

The Meanings of Saturn in Traditional Astrology

- Borders delineate and separate us, so Saturn is aloneness, isolation, being confined in a border or structure. Part of life in time includes fragmentation into separate entities. We are no longer simply part of oneness, we are separate beings.

- Saturn relates to habit, which is a structure that is built from repeated action over time, an action like a groove that has its own momentum.

- In Aristotle the virtues are described as habits we need to build by repeated actions, so Saturn can also be discipline, creating good habits. Saturn can also be the inertia of long standing bad habits, and their consequences.

Cold and Damp - This is an early attribution that is likely related to being opposite the Sun, and to Saturn being connected with Winter. This includes rotting, decaying, which combines cold and damp with time. Saturn is linked to Winter, and old age and dying are the winter of a human life.

Law and Judgment - This is a rich association, related to Saturn as structure, and to Saturn as at the border of time and eternal. Hence Saturn mirrors the eternal laws and structures into time.

- This relates to judgment, the consequences of action.

- Moral and religious wisdom relate to knowledge and understanding of the laws. Thus we also get the connection with profundity and depth of thought.

- Saturn ties to duty, which is the obligation to learn and follow the moral laws.

- Law plus age gives tradition passed down. Thus, for instance, Saturn strong in the ninth house can indicate interest in traditional philosophy and astrology.

- Saturn relates to the virtues of humility and selfless service. If the Sun is affirmation of the self then Saturn is the negation. If

The Meanings of Saturn in Traditional Astrology

Sun is egotism then Saturn is humility. Combine with duty to law and you get selfless service.

- Relate this to feelings of guilt, shame, fear, related to a moral law and the knowledge one has broken it.

- Consequences and judgment connect the concepts of law with time.

- In a larger sense Saturn is fate, fortune, providence, those things that happen to you because of the laws playing out over time.

- Saturn gives perspective, objectivity, which combines time with law with thought.

- With time you get a sense of history, of passage of time.

Opposition - Many of the meanings of Saturn are related to this basic aspect from the Thema Mundi where Saturn is in opposition to the Sun. Hence we get Saturn as adversary, opposer, that which blocks, hinders. Delay is opposition over time.

Here are other meanings of Saturn, with some thoughts as to how they were derived from the core meanings we looked at.

Lowly, Poor, Despised - Saturn as low as opposed to Sun as high. This also can mean physically low, hence places underground like caves, or basements in buildings. This combines being low with being dark and hidden, and possibly cold and damp.

Deceitful, Cynical - Think of Saturn opposite Sun, which is wide open, visible and honest. Saturn in turn can be hidden, deliberately hiding or deceiving.

Evil, Malefic, Harmful - This is related to Saturn opposite the lights, and Saturn as opposition, so we have evil as opposition to good, separated off or in rebellion from the good. Malefic and moral evil aren't quite the same thing, and we will look at those concepts in more detail in a later essay.

All of these clusters of meaning of Saturn relate to just a couple of main starting points - Saturn as opposite the Sun and furthest from the Sun, and Saturn as the outermost planet on the border of time and eternity. These seem to be the main keys to Saturn's meaning.

Transition Astrologers

These next two astrologers I quote are from the 1800's. They are not yet quite part of the modern era, but at the same time we can see that a lot of the richness of meaning of the traditional texts is being lost. We also see the beginning of the move away from physical and concrete meanings towards primarily psychology and character description.

Take into account that both of the astrologers I look at in this section are late 18th century, the era of Darwin and evolution, the era of spiritualism and theosophy. We are right at the border of the change to modern astrology here.

Raphael Guide to Astrology

This book was first published in 1877. Raphael is a British astrologer, or rather a series of astrologers who wrote with this pseudonym.

It is very noteworthy that this is essentially the same sort of description that we see in the very earliest Hellenistic material. The general associations and themes are recognizably the same. Traditional astrology stayed remarkably conservative and consistent throughout most of its history. It is only in the twentieth century and later than we start seeing significant changes in meaning.

As compared to the previous lists of significations, these are almost all character traits, although we do see attributions to external things and events in the section on Saturn through the houses. Description of planets is by house position. I will first give the description for the Ascendant since it is the longest, and then a sample of meanings for other houses.

> This planet in the Ascendant at birth makes the native timid, cautious, mistrustful, and fearful: reserved, thoughtful, malicious and revengeful; covetous and envious.
>
> In the fiery signs he is improved; he is more free, straight, and honest in his actions, but rash and impetuous, fond of argument and quarreling.
>
> In the earthy signs, especially Taurus, the native is sottish, dull, heavy and malicious; in Virgo very inquisitive, suspicious and fretful; in Capricorn argumentative, crafty, selfish, hard-working and miserly. In the airy signs, thoughtful, studious, contemplative, close over money matters and his own affairs, sincere and devout in religion so far as it concerns "self".

Gemini and Aquarius are better signs than Libra, for in the latter he is simply a nuisance to every one on account of his opinionative, selfish, miserly, and proud ways.

In Cancer or Pisces especially, he is dull, sottish, and dejected, depraved, and obscene; sometimes an enthusiast in religion; in Scorpio very crafty and malicious and not to be trusted.

Generally the native of Saturn is shy, and has aversion to his own ends; miserly, fond of his habitation; constant, curious in religious beliefs, fanciful and bigoted, frequently an impediment in speech (except Saturn be in the airy signs), careful of his affairs and family, austere and averse to changes.

Saturn in the 2nd - Much trouble and worry in money matters; loss of money; ill success in trade or business; the native has usually to work very hard for his money, even when Saturn is essentially fortified; when out of dignities, distress and poverty usually dog the native's footsteps, more or less through life.

Saturn in the 9th - Firm and steadfast in religion; headstrong, thoughtful, reserved, and contemplative; studious; fond of astrology, occultism, and things out of the common track, magic, &c., danger in traveling by water; loss through relations by marriage. The native should avoid foreign lands unless Saturn be very strong by position or aspect.

Saturn in the 10th - Success in life, with an ultimate fall to disgrace and trouble; frequent discredit in business; trouble to the mother and loss of substance.

Sepharial, The Manual of Astrology

Sepharial, or Walter Orn Gold, is another influential British astrologer who wrote under a pseudonym. The section on the planets in this book consists of reference tables by topic, similar to Al-Biruni. The lists are much more abbreviated. When you get to the house meanings we are starting to see more of an emphasis on personal qualities and experience. It is consistent with the earlier lists, but much abbreviated. The connection with cold, heavy, dark and dry is constant, the connection with water is pretty much gone. This reads like a condensed digest of previous texts.

> [TEMPERAMENT] Saturn is nervous, secretive, defensive, binding, constant, cold, dry, hard and barren.
>
> [FLAVOURS] Saturn is cold, astringent and sour.
>
> [FORMS] Saturn gives hard, clear-cut outlines, straight short lines, and cramped forms.
>
> [COLOURS] Saturn: black, dark brown, and indigo.
>
> [METALS] Saturn governs lead.
>
> [PARTS OF HUMAN BODY] Saturn rules over bones and articulations, liver, spleen, left ear, the calves and knees; the secretive system generally.
>
> [OCCUPATIONS] Saturn - Land and property dealers, miners, coal merchants, dealers in lead and other Saturnine commodities, plumbers, jailers, sextons, grave-diggers, watchmen etc.; such as follow laborious employments, and those that work at night or underground.

Here are some examples of the meanings of Saturn in the houses.

First House: Saturn - Melancholy mind, solitary habits; shy, nervous manners; subjects the native to colds; causes bruises to the head; an uphill struggle; patient disposition.

Second House: Saturn - Business losses; a thrifty nature; hard work for little gain; sometimes poverty.

Ninth House: Saturn - Taste for philosophy; religious spirit; troubles in foreign lands; dangerous voyages; loss through legal suits; deceit among relatives by marriage; studious and thoughtful nature.

Tenth House: Saturn - Rise in life, followed by a downfall. Patience and firmness of purpose mark the life of the native. In business, financial ruin is shown; in professional life, dishonour and failure; in government, defeat. A fatality hangs over the native from his birth; danger of ruin or loss of a parent in early life; public affairs fail or bring to loss and discredit.

The Old and New Cosmos

In order to understand the meanings given to Saturn in the twentieth century we need to realize that the modern model of the universe is very different from the traditional model. We have seen that that there is a notable consistency in the meanings attributed to Saturn throughout the traditional era, from the Hellenistic period up through the 17th century and the era of William Lilly. That same era shared a notable consistency in world view, including the periods of the Greek and Roman civilizations, the Judeo-Christian civilization, and the Islamic civilization, all of which have a common heritage. For all the differences and developments there are notable stable consistencies in the shape of their world, things they took for granted that we have a hard time conceiving today.

We have a differently shaped world in our minds today; when we look out at the world in the early 21st century we do not see the same kind of world that our ancestors saw. This affects how we think, how we feel, how we speak and act - and, how we conceive of astrology, and the meanings we give to the elements of astrology.

This does not mean that the Universe has changed, it means that our conception of the Universe has changed. This does not mean that our modern conception is improved, or truer, or more evolved. It means that it is different. And, it emphatically does not mean that we are smarter or more evolved than our ancestors.

Over the past few centuries there have been a series of discoveries and developments that have completely changed how we view the world we live in. We will briefly review some of these and their contribution to our changed world.

The Solar System

There is a significant change in our conception of the solar system and galaxy. In the old model the earth is a fixed center, with the planets revolving around the earth, and then the fixed and eternal firmament of heaven with the fixed stars outside of the spheres of the planets.

This began to change in the 15th and 16th centuries, with the work of Copernicus and Galileo demonstrating that it makes more sense mathematically to view the Earth and other planets as revolving around the Sun, rather than having the Earth be the static center of the cosmos. In our modern world it is hard to conceive what a traumatic shift this must have been. The stable and unchanging order of the world was knocked askew, and what was once the fixed center was set in motion.

More recently there has been a further shift. Along with the earth revolving around the Sun, we now have a larger frame of reference, where our entire solar system is itself in motion moving through the galaxy, revolving around a point referred to as the galactic center.

Our ancestors looked up at the sky and saw a fixed and eternal order, the firmament of heaven, an enclosed dome or arch like a grand cathedral. It is a grand, stable, unmoving and eternal order mirrored in the heavens. By contrast, in our modern world we look up - or, rather, we look out - and see moving, endless infinite space. That is a profound change in perspective. We live in a world in movement and in perpetual flux, with nothing outside of it. This loss of any fixed and eternal standard in our modern world will resonate through almost all of the changes in our worldview that we are considering here here.

New Planets

Parallel with this change in the cosmos, Saturn in the modern era is no longer considered to be the outermost planet. There have been new planets discovered - first Uranus in 1781, then Neptune in 1846. Pluto was considered to be a planet when it was first discovered in 1930.

Even though Pluto has lost its official status as a planet in modern science, it is still effectively a planet in most of modern astrology, and it plays a prominent role in some schools.

Saturn is no longer the outermost planet in modern astrology, and it no longer sits at the outer border of the moving planets, at the edge of the sphere of the fixed stars. In the old order Saturn stood at the border between time and eternity, and in the new cosmos it is one more moving body in the midst of other moving bodies.

We will see, as we consider more modern astrologers, that this has a very profound effect on changing concepts of the meaning of the planet Saturn. Traditional astrologers (like myself) have a very different conception of the three modern outer planets than do most modern astrologers. Traditional astrologers also typically approach the meaning of Saturn and the other classical seven planets in a different way from many modern astrologers.

Ancient and Modern Science

Parallel with this change in the cosmos is the rise of what we call the modern scientific worldview. It is materialist, viewing the universe as basically created from matter, and all other elements growing from that, including different forms of life, and eventually humans. Human consciousness has a somewhat precarious place in this model.

I am simplifying here to paint a picture, but I think the broad strokes are accurate. In the old concept of the world there is an eternal order, and usually the concept of an eternal Creator and ruler of that order, and the changing world we live in here on earth is within that eternal order. The traditional order is top down, starting with the eternal and concluding with matter, and the new order is bottom-up starting with matter and growing upward.

There were different notions as to how humans could learn that traditional order. Following Aristotle, some thought that we learn from sense experience, and then we abstract or draw out principles of order from that. Others, following Plato and his school, thought that we have these principles of order inherent in our minds, and our sense experience is needed to bring those to awareness.

Either way there is an assumption that there is a basic order that is there and that is real, and that our minds can apprehend that order. God or the Divine, the external world, and the world of the human mind, are all of a piece and all correspond with each other.

The old order of the cosmos is fixed, eternal and ordered, from the top down - as it was in the beginning, is now, and ever shall be, world without end. The new order is changing, growing, evolving from the bottom up, with no boundaries and no fixed order.

Science Old and New

Most people don't realize that the meaning and connotations of the term Science have changed greatly in the past few hundred years. In the older meaning of the term, Science is primarily based on eternal and unchanging laws and principles. We can think of these laws completely separate from sense experience, and these laws exist independent of external sense experience. We can think directly about what is real and true since these are mirrored in our minds. Note that this internal abstract order includes an ethical dimension, so that when we think of concepts like Justice, this corresponds to something real. By contrast, in the modern meaning of the term, Science is now based strictly on observation and empirical evidence.

This shift in the meaning of the term Science is very recent, within about the last 150 years. If you go back and look at the original Webster's dictionary from the early 1800's the older meaning of the term still dominates. That old definition has completely disappeared from more modern dictionaries, and the strictly empirical sense fits how we usually use the term today. I have included an essay in the Appendix where I examine older dictionary definitions and examples to illustrate that.

There is a very good chance that, when you read the paragraph on the old meaning of the term science, that either it did not register, or it sounded kind of odd, or perhaps you weren't quite sure what it meant. You very likely thought something like, "*Well goodness, everyone knows that Science means empirical evidence!*" **That is exactly what I mean when I talk about assumptions we take for granted and likely do not even notice. This is what the word Science means to us today, so we assume that it always meant that.**

Evolution and Progress

These are other modern concepts that took shape around the same time to combine with this changing model of the world. Our model of the cosmos has changed, how we think of Science has changed, and parallel to that is a huge shift in how we think of the origin and place of the human race in this new order.

Charles Darwin published his *On the Origin of Species* in 1859, and since then his concept of evolution, starting with simpler elements and moving towards more complex, has become a dominant metaphor shaping how we think of the world, a metaphor that goes far beyond Darwin's original scientific claims.

During this same time period we have an era of rapid technological invention and progress, largely driven by the use of our planet's fossil fuels, first coal, and then oil and gas. This provided a metaphor of progress that combines with the metaphor of evolution to give a picture of an endless march of improvement moving ever forward and upward from the past to the future.

This in turn parallels the peak of the period of European and British colonial expansion and domination across the entire earth, a growth which was viewed at the time as the growth and spread of civilization, moving the entire human race forward with it. The concepts of evolution and progress are now linked with the concept of endless expansion. This applies to our now endless and infinite solar system, and it applies to the growth of modern civilization across the planet.

Progress equals evolution equals growth equals expansion - all of these concepts are now linked in our minds. They are now so much a part of our view of the world that we don't see them anymore. They are assumptions, perceptual filters, as much a part of our environment as the air we breathe. Our ancestors looked at the sky and saw a fixed eternal order. We look up and see potential, boundless and limitless possibility for endless growth and expansion. To quote a slogan from a popular TV show, we are ready to Boldly Go Where No Man Has Gone Before.

Past and Future

An important effect of this new metaphor is to place a great value on the new over the old, the future over the past. If there is constant evolution and improvement then the past must be outmoded, and the future promises new glories. The past is devalued, the new and modern is highly valued.

In the old order a high value was placed on tradition, the wisdom of the past, which was thought to reflect an eternal unchanging order. In the new world the past is superseded by the present, the old fashioned by the modern, the primitive and superstitious past by the enlightened and superior future. We make many of our value judgments in the context of this model, and it permeates much of astrology writing from the twentieth century on forward.

I cannot emphasize this point enough.

This underlying assumption that new is better than old and future is better than past is deeply embedded in how we look at the world today, so much so that it is very difficult to become conscious of its all-pervasive scope. We will see that assumption repeatedly as we look at the writings of twentieth century astrologers.

The Concept of Changing Truth

If the universe is constantly evolving and improving, this means that our ideas about the universe must also be evolving and improving. You get the interesting notion that truth itself is malleable, and changes with the time. So, for instance, the Medieval philosopher Thomas Aquinas may have been the pinnacle of thinking about the truth for his time, but his thought is now outmoded, old-fashioned. It is old, therefore it can no longer be true. Many modern people have a hard time conceiving how Aquinas could be relevant to our modern age when so much has changed. Truth itself has become plastic, changing, and New Truth is superior to Old Truth by the very fact that it is New.

This underlying assumption is also very pervasive in much modern astrology writing. There is the unspoken, and sometimes spoken, assumption that our new astrology is superior, cutting-edge, and that it supersedes the quaint and superstitious ways of the old astrologers. This also means that modern astrologers often approach their work with the idea that they have to come up with something new - that they need a fresh way of looking at things - that they can discard many of the outmoded old ways and replace them with superior new ways. There is a high value placed on innovation and originality, so you see more innovation in the meanings of astrology in the last one hundred years than in the previous two thousand.

Is this change a positive thing? If you live in a world that assumes perpetual progress, the answer is yes. **That is an assumption and not a truth, so it is worth becoming aware of and questioning that assumption.**

Theosophy and Eastern Philosophy

At around the same time that Darwin's metaphor of evolution was taking hold, we see the growth of the Theosophical movement in the late 19th century, largely pioneered by Madame Blavatsky. Theosophy has had an enormous influence on modern astrology and it was very influential in the astrology "revival", or rather the re-invention of astrology in the 20th century.

Blavatsky and Theosophy drew on Eastern spiritual models, and it is through Theosophy that the concepts of reincarnation, multiple lives and karma became part of the spiritual vocabulary of our culture in general and astrology specifically.

Blavatsky was very much a child of her times, and the Hindu concepts of karma and multiple lives across endless aeons was combined with the notion of evolution and progress. Taken by itself the Hindu concepts of cycles were just that, cyclical, and revolved in an endless wheel. What we have today is a hybrid notion of endless cycles that are also progressing, moving forward and expanding. Theosophy combined Hindu cosmology with Darwin to give us a kind of religion of ongoing spiritual progress through an endless series of lives, a process of limitless expansion which culminates in union with the Infinite Divine.

Positive Thinking and New Thought

Right around this same time period of the late 1800's, when Darwin's concept of evolution was turning the intellectual and spiritual worlds on their heads, and Theosophy was beginning exert its influence on modern culture, we have the flowering of another modern school that strongly influences all of twentieth century thought up to the present day. It was originally known as New Thought, or as Christian Science or Science of Mind, and today we are more likely to conceive of it as Positive Thinking. This is the movement that is based on the idea that our thinking can effect our reality - not just our mood or state of mind, but our physical health and well-being, and even our external environment.

While the mind was conquering the world technologically through science, and the mind was evolving to greater power and capability through evolution, and expanding to new spiritual levels with Theosophy, it only makes sense that there should be a parallel sense of discovery of the power of human thought to shape reality. This was expressed through mind healing movements like Christian Science; in movements espousing prosperity through right thinking like Napoleon Hill's *Think and Grow Rich*; through the general positive attitude of Norman Vincent Peale's *The Power of Positive Thinking*, and finally through to its logical conclusion in the New Age slogan and core belief, You Create Your Own Reality.

You can see how this belief in the power of mind can tie in with evolution, with progress (scientific and otherwise), through limitless expansion smashing through previous barriers, through expansion into outer space - and through limitless spiritual expansion and evolution across a limitless series of lives. There is a great sense of infatuation, even a kind of drunken giddiness, to this sense of the limitless power of the human mind.

This core belief in the power of positive thinking pervades almost all aspects of our modern culture, for good or for ill. Not surprisingly it also is a hallmark of much modern astrology, which has a very strong emphasis on interpreting everything in the chart in a positive way, on looking for potential, and on giving virtually unlimited power to the individual human, through effort and positive mental discipline, to make what they will of the potential of the natal chart, or of progressions, or of transits. Our astrology chart is potential, and it is ours to develop and do with as we will.

Values and Ethics

If God is dead, if there is no eternal fixed heaven to look up to, if truth itself can change and evolve, then logically there are no fixed and eternal moral standards either. Morality becomes a matter of subjective feeling, opinion and judgment. Moral standards can also evolve, grow and change, and yesterday's moral laws are no longer normative for today's world. The tablets of the Ten Commandments have been shattered.

Values are now considered relative, and depend on your point of view. There is no longer The Truth, there is now My Truth, and Your Truth - and who am I, who is anyone to say that My Truth is superior to yours? At first glance this can seem to be very liberating. There is no more abiding by old outmoded moral standards, no more guilt and sin, and each of us is free to choose our reality for ourselves, to become who we want to be.

Again, this can sound liberating and generous at first glance, but I maintain that, if you really think through the implications of this belief, that this is one of the most dangerous and destructive movements in modern culture - dangerous enough that, pushed to its logical conclusion, it will destroy western civilization. This is important enough that I will devote a separate chapter to this topic later in the book.

Thinking and Feeling

Human reason is our ability to make judgments, to weigh, compare and contrast different ideas and evidence to come to a conclusion. It is a distinctly human trait, one that sets us aside from any other known living creatures. For most of human history the overwhelming majority of humanity assumed that there is a fixed and eternal reality, physical, moral and spiritual, that provides an eternal guideline, an eternal standard to judge by. There is a World Out There that our minds have to conform to.

When there no longer is an eternal standard, then human reason needs to look somewhere for a basis to make judgments. Reason all by itself cannot measure anything unless it has something to measure by. With no external standard to look to, reason turns within - and the effective basis of judgment is now feeling, emotion. The important thing about a judgment is that it feels right. This is very nearly the inverse of the traditional model of the human, where the task of human reason is to shape, direct and grow the human emotional life to conform to moral standards. With no standards, reason is now shaped by feeling rather than the other way around. The world is changing, our reason no longer has a solid base to build on, so our only guide is our subjective feelings.

Modern Psychology

We already talked about some important movements all converging around the end of the 1800's - Theosophy, Darwin's concept of evolution, scientific and technological progress, and the expansion of western civilization across the globe. During this same period we have the emergence of the work of Sigmund Freud, of the concept of the unconscious mind, and of psychoanalysis. Freud's one-time student and colleague Carl Jung took this work further, and Jung's work has had an enormous influence on the development of 20th century astrology from about mid-century onwards.

To many in the modern world God was dead, the Heavens were gone, and they were replaced by the limitless reaches of the human mind within. The exploration and expansion of inner space paralleled the expansion into outer space. God, the angels and the spiritual world were replaced by the archetypes of the collective unconscious. The worship of God has been replaced with worship of the human and of human potential. The human being is now the measure of all things, and the human mind recognizes no superior power. There are no external restrictions that the human cannot smash through to free itself. Reality is whatever the human decides it should be by its own power to shape the world.

Inner-Outer Disconnect

There is one more important element in the modern world view, an element that goes at least as far back as Rene Descartes in the 16th and 17th centuries, the same era as William Lilly, and of Copernicus and Galileo. In the traditional world the human mind and the outer existing universe are all of a piece, and when we think of the world, our thought has a real correspondence with something existing. In the modern worldview there is a disconnect between the subjective world of human consciousness and the external material world.

With this disconnect, it now means that all value judgments and all ethical judgments are strictly subjective and exist only within the human mind. The external world of matter, the world studied by our modern science, is strictly value-free. It is mere sense data to us, and any value it has it projected onto it by the human mind.

Values exist only within human consciousness. They have no real external referent.

This points to the single most striking and pervasive difference in the descriptions of the meaning of Saturn, or of astrology in general, in the traditional texts compared to the modern writing. We are so thoroughly used to this change that it is easy to miss it.

In the traditional texts the majority of the attributions are of things existing outside the human mind - places, animals, trees, herbs, weather, and so on. In most modern texts the overwhelming majority of the descriptions are of attributes of human consciousness.

You will sometimes see modern astrologers describe the old astrology as fatalistic. I suspect this change is part of what they are getting at. The old astrology includes the whole world, including all kinds of factors out of our control. Much of the new modern astrology is almost exclusively within our minds and refers only to things we can control.

The emphasis in modern astrology on character analysis rather than external prediction also has a legal background. Most countries had strict laws against fortune telling, and Alan Leo, one of the most prominent and influential early 20th century philosophers, was brought to court multiple times for violating these laws. Part of the way Leo dealt with this was to switch the emphasis in his writing from prediction to psychology and character. That has had an enormous influence on the further development of astrology in the 20th century.

Summing Up - The New World

This brief survey of the changes in our modern way of looking at the world has a couple of main purposes. The first is to to show the many ways that our modern way of looking at the world is very different from the world of traditional astrology. Second, and more important, is to bring to mind and make conscious some of the very important assumptions that we in the modern world take for granted without being aware of them at all.

In the following sections, where we examine the writing about Saturn by astrologers of the twentieth century and later, I will be focusing in my comments on the kinds of assumptions the authors are making, likely without being completely aware that they are just that, assumptions.

The main purpose of the following sections on modern astrologers is not to find fault, it is to bring assumptions to conscious awareness. The only time I criticize modern astrologers is when I think they unfairly caricature traditional astrology in order to belittle or dismiss it.

I will note that I am only including astrologers that I admire, who have done or are doing good and worthwhile work from their particular point of view. I never criticize or comment on anyone who I do not first respect. Also, I am trying to include examples of astrologers from different schools, using very different approaches. There is a great deal of variety in modern astrology, far more than in any of the previous history of western traditional astrology. Note that I am dealing only with Western astrology here. I do not have enough familiarity with what is called Vedic astrology or Jyotish to comment intelligently on that tradition.

Throughout this section I will be applying the Chesterton Test, taking statements that use vague or technical sounding words and restating them in plain, blunt ordinary language. This is to help us see what is actually being said so that we can think about it and examine it.

Max Heindel

Max Heindel (1865-1919) was an astrologer and the founder of the Rosicrucian Fellowship at Oceanside, California. Heindel's school was a Christianized descendant of Theosophy. His text on drawing up a chart, **Simplified Scientific Astrology**, was very popular in the middle 20th century and served as a starting textbook for many astrologers, including me. The quotes here are from his basic text on astrology's meaning, **The Message of the Stars**.

In this first section Heindel is focusing on Saturn as opposed to the Sun, looking at opposites. Note the very strong moralistic tone, and how it puts the planet in the overall frame of the evolution of our souls towards unselfishness. We also see a very heavy emphasis on karma and multiple lives, so that anything bad that happens to us is our own fault and is punishment. We really don't see that thread in the meanings of Saturn prior to Theosophy and the twentieth century, and it now dominates much of modern astrology. This also implies that whatever bad happens is because of something within us, another theme that permeates much of modern astrology.

Finally, notice that much of the concrete detail, the listings of attributions, has pretty much dropped away. The interpretation is less concrete, more abstract, more conceptual.

> Life manifests as motion; but the keynote of Saturn is Obstruction, therefore that is the planet of decrepitude and decay, and consequently when the Sun is in Libra, the sign of Saturn's exaltation, at the fall equinox, Nature is tired and ready for its wintry sleep.
>
> In youth, when the Sun's forces surge through the frame, assimilation and excretion balance, but as time goes on, "Chronos" or Saturn accumulates obstructions in the organs of secretion, and elimination is gradually restricted, the avenues of life are dammed up, and decrepitude and

decay turn the scales of life (Libra) towards the realm of death.

Similarly in other departments of life; where the Sun makes the social favorite, by imbuing him with optimism and a bright sunny smile, Saturn makes recluses and sours existence with frowns and pessimism...

The leash of Saturn is not pleasant; we sometimes chafe, fret and fume while being thus held in leash; but meanwhile we are ripened and are more fitted, when the obstruction is removed, to have or use that which Saturn delayed, for as we develop physical muscle by overcoming physical obstacles, so we cultivate soul power by the resistance spiritually engendered by Saturn.

When we remember that the destiny shown by our horoscope is of our own making in past existences then we shall understand that Saturn only marks the weak spots in our horoscope, where we are vulnerable and liable to go wrong. When the weak points have been brought out through temptation, *and we have yielded*, the punishment follows automatically as a natural and logical sequence, for every wrong act carries in itself the seed of punishment which brings home to our consciousness the mistakes we have made. We must hold clearly before our mind's eye that though the planets incline to a certain line of action we, as evolving Egos, are supposed to discriminate between good and evil and choose only that which is good. If we fail in this respect and *yield* to the temptation the transgression merits a just recompense under the laws of nature and these are the things signified by Saturn.

Tact and diplomacy, method and system, patience and perseverance, honor and chastity, industry and mechanical ability, justice and fair-mindedness all come from Saturn when he is well-aspected and it is only when we transgress the principles for which he stands that under the influences generated by his adverse aspects he punishes us until he has brought us to our knees to pray to our Father in Heaven for forgiveness and strength to overcome our lower nature.

Llewellyn George

Llewellyn George (1876-1954) was the founder of Llewellyn Publications. His massive textbook, **A to Z Horoscope Maker and Delineator**, was one of the most comprehensive and useful overall astrology texts for much of the century. The quotes here are from the original edition, which I think is much superior to the greatly revised edition currently available.

This book was first published in 1910. Llewellyn George is an interesting bridge figure, and he keeps a lot of the old attributions while combining them with some of the Theosophical and positive thinking approach.

> Saturn - Sometimes symbolized as Father Time. In olden days Sater, or Satan was its name and it signified evil, darkness, secrecy, loss and misfortune. Its nature is cold, dry, phlegmatic, earthly and masculine. When Saturn is well placed or aspected, the person, is grave, profound, prudent, cautious and of excellent organizing and executive ability. But when he is weak or afflicted, the native is apt to be bigoted, acquisitive, irritable, discontented and complaining. He governs the teeth, bones, spleen, knees, right ear, and sense of hearing. Rules bricklaying, pottery, masonry, plumbing and other laborious or uncongenial employment. Denotes aged persons, thin, nervous, dark, seclusive. Also farmers, miners; coal, junk or produce dealers, property owners. It rules land, property, mines, lead and dealings in real estate.

Here we have the earliest reference I have found associating Saturn with Satan, the devil. We did not see this explicit association the earlier texts, but it is very common in modern works on Saturn, and we will note it repeatedly in the following chapters. Most of the rest of the paragraph is the sort of list of attributes we have seen repeatedly in traditional texts.

Llewellyn George

This next set of quotes is from a section on Saturn in the 12 signs.

> The influence of Saturn is commonly called evil, and in this respect he is much maligned as in reality there is no evil, since all things work together for good ultimately. Saturn acts as a deterrent and because he brings denial and necessity into some lives, has been considered an oppressor or Satan. "He that filleth with pride will suffer a fall," for Saturn will bring him to his knees, humble his nature, and by means of restrictions, limitations and adversities, will cause the individual to ponder, study and seek to find the source of woe, that in future it may be overcome. Thus, while Saturn is a destroyer (of false ideals), he is also a redeemer, in that he brings the mind to a state of introspection and stimulates effort toward perfection and victory.
>
> Persons born with Saturn well placed and aspected in their horoscope have a serious and practical nature; they are wisely economical, prudent, conservative, executive and profound, being good organizers and managers.

In this section Llewellyn George sounds very similar to the quotes we looked at from Max Heindel. The moralistic, multiple lifetime viewpoint of Theosophy dominates.

Charles E O Carter

Charles Ernest Owen Carter (1887-1968) was a prominent and influential astrologer and Theosophist who wrote a series of basic astrology texts that were very influential in the middle 20th century. In these quotes from Carter there is still a consistency with the previous traditional meanings, but also note that the description is streamlined, and is framed more in terms of both moral and spiritual purpose and of psychological traits. The highlighted words are Carter's, and they are along the lines of the approach that sums up the meaning of a planet in a few keywords. This approach is very popular in modern texts.

> This body rules Aquarius, fixed air, and Capricorn, cardinal earth. It is exalted in Libra, wherein it becomes gentler and more merciful, for of itself Saturn is the planet of strict justice that demands full payment for all it bestows. It is the **planet of the concrete and practical**, and gives a vivid sense of material values and what are called hard facts. When strong it gives most of the virtues of what may be called the "self-help" type, such as patience, perseverance, hard work, thrift, concentration, solidity, and reliability.
>
> It is the planet of **limitation**, and even when well placed in the horoscope the native who comes much under its ray is apt to be limited and circumscribed in his views and sympathies, conservative, cautious, and narrow.
>
> When ill-placed as regards sign and aspect, but prominent by house, it is apt to show meanness, selfishness, a sense of heavy responsibilities, and a despondent, sad outlook. In this respect it may be contrasted with the three fiery planets (my note - Sun, Mars, Jupiter) and their typical optimism and faith - in God, luck or themselves, according to their stage of moral evolution. The true Saturnian usually believes that nothing can be won without hard

work, and he has both the virtues and vices of this belief. It is the planet of real worth, as apart from show and make-believe, and gives to all things their permanent and lasting qualities. On the other hand, by limiting the outgoing activities of fire, it causes checks, delays, and disappointments, and so becomes the planet of fate, which sets definite bounds to our efforts.

Its action is slow, thorough, and inevitable.

The Only Way to Learn Astrology

This is excerpted from the first book of a series of textbooks with this title by Marion March and Joan McEvers. This was a very popular series in the 1970's and after, and is still in print and widely available. The approach in this book is thoroughly psychological and keyword driven. The description starts with line giving a symbolic meaning to the glyph of Saturn, something we did not see in the traditional texts.

> glyph; sickle of Chronos, the God of Time.

The mythology of Saturn gets traced back to different figures by different people. In Greek mythology, Kronus, husband of Rhea and father of Zeus/Jupiter, is a different god than Chronos, related to Time, and the two were conflated when referring to Saturn. This is the one place that I have seen the Saturn glyph described as the sickle of the Reaper. They do not mention that the sickle is also typically associated with the figure of Death as the Grim Reaper, and as far as I can tell they do not mention the connection of Saturn with death. Saturn has largely lost its association with death in much of modern astrology.

> anatomy: the skin, the skeletal system (including the teeth), ligaments, knees, the left ear and auditory organs, gall bladder, parathyroid glands, body protein.

> represents **urge for security and safety**

Notice she takes the meaning of Saturn and encapsulates it as referring to a single psychological urge. If you think back on the wide range of associations we saw in the various traditional texts, there really aren't that many that are directly related to security and safety. This is taking a single aspect of Saturn - as boundary, border - and turning it into a psychological urge to have a safe place, a safe boundary, a safe refuge to hide in.

> keyword **the teacher**

This sums up the effect of Saturn in a single word, and it is a very different concept from security and safety. This is picking up a thread of Saturn as the wisdom of experience, learning in the school of hard knocks.

> Rules form, discipline, responsibility, organization, ambition, capacity for a career, limitations, sorrows and delays. Saturn rules theories and scientific law, older persons, depth, patience, timing, tradition, conventionality, orthodoxy and productive use of time. Saturn represents the principles of truth, of contraction, of solidification, of wisdom and aging. Its action is slow and lasting. Saturn is the taskmaster of the horoscope. In earlier times it was known as the **greater malefic. Where you find Saturn in the horoscope is where you feel least secure and tend to overcompensate.**

Saturn here shows a desire for security - but it is where you feel insecure. The implication here is that you only experience bad fortune where you feel insecure - and that is just not the case. Also note the 20th century characteristic of describing the planets as psychological traits, ways you act and feel. Notice that she did not mention corruption, decay, disease and death, or deceit, or hiddenness. There are many, many traditional aspects of Saturn symbolism that were omitted here.

This next section continues the late 20th century theme of setting Uranus over against Saturn. I am quoting from the meanings attributed to Uranus as these end up profoundly changing the meanings attributed to Saturn.

> (Uranus)
>
> represents **freedom urge ("divine discontent")**
>
> keyword **the awakener**

> It is futuristic, humanitarian, intellectual... it governs, revolution, rebellions and autonomy... Uranus is a breaker of traditions.

The traditions that Uranus rebels against, the old evil restrictions, end up being associated with Saturn. This pairing is ubiquitous in modern astrology.

Ronald Davison

Ronald C Davison (1914-1985) was a prominent British astrologer. His popular astrology textbooks were designed to be very concise and practical in approach.

Instead of the list of various attributes we saw in traditional texts, the planets are here described by their function, what job are they preforming. Also note that the function refers to a process of evolution or perfection of character. Note also Saturn is interpreted as being external, which is opposed to Uranus as internal.

Note that all the Capitalized Words in the Following Quotes are as in the Original Text.

> Saturn is the Tester (Satan) whose function is to perfect character through constant trials. The rings of Saturn symbolize the limitations imposed by Saturnian action that operate as a harsh external discipline until we have learned to discipline ourselves.

Again, note defining a planet as having a title and a function. This is one of the first places I have seen where Saturn's rings are given any symbolic meaning. Also note the implication that we experience Saturn as harsh UNTIL we learn to discipline ourselves. The assumption is that whatever harsh happens is our fault, due to our lack of discipline.

This is a typical mid to late 20th century approach. In this approach the potential in the chart is all good, and we are destined for good fortune and success IF we do it right - and we suffer, and experience bad fortune, where we do it wrong. Now to be fair I question whether Davison himself would put things quite that bluntly if you confronted him with it, but I maintain that is indeed the implication of his description.

> It represents the principle of Contraction, Crystallization, Concentration, the ability to impose Limits; Ambition,

> Self-Preservation, Conventionality, Caution, Pessimism, Sense of Lack, Integrity, Responsibility, Justice, Perseverance, Stability, Endurance.
>
> It represents Time as a crystallization of Eternity. Saturn, or Satan, is thus shown as the enemy of God, who dwells in Eternity.

As we noted previously it is only in the twentieth century that we get the equation of Saturn and Satan, the Devil, enemy of God. Also notice that the implication is that Time and Eternity are opposites, enemies. They are indeed different levels of existence in traditional astrology, but I do not think you would find time and eternity set up as enemies, and I think that is implied here.

> Saturn is the planet of old age, where the life processes are slowed up. It signifies old or serious people, the father, those in responsible positions, farmers, builders, civil servants.
>
> Its action is to limit, conserve, test, deepen, perfect, inhibit, delay, restrict.
>
> It rules the negative Capricorn, where material organization and practical ambition reaches its peak, and the positive Aquarius, where detachment is paramount. Its fall is in Cancer, where it becomes hypersensitive, and Leo, where its ambition is boundless. It is exalted in Libra, showing exact Justice perfectly balanced. It is in detriment in Aries, where impetuosity is the enemy of Stability. Its glyph shows the cross of matter elevated above the crescent of receptivity, symbolically placed at the Nadir (assimilation, pull of the past.)
>
> (Section on Uranus) This planet acts to break up the crystallizations of Saturn. It represents Originality, Inspiration, Dynamic Self-Expression, Independence...

Here is our Hero Uranus again. The meanings of Saturn have been redefined based on this next planet out. This is a profound shift in meaning, one we will discuss further in some of the later essays.

Isabel Hickey

James Holden describes Isabel Hickey (1903-1980) as an "American astrologer, author and teacher, well-known in the Boston area." I am quoting from her book **Astrology: A Cosmic Science** as a good and characteristic example of 20th century spiritual astrology.

Spiritual astrology is an example of a wider 20th century phenomenon where we see different forms of astrology which are combined with other disciplines or subjects. For instance, there is spiritual astrology; there is psychological astrology, including the very popular Jungian astrology; there is archetypal astrology, and Uranian astrology, and evolutionary astrology, and harmonic astrology. More recently you have queer astrology, and feminist astrology, and pagan astrology, and probably social justice astrology, and so on.

With these different schools astrology itself loses its distinctness as a discipline, and it becomes a vehicle to be used to further the agenda of its parent. For instance, psychological astrology puts the Jungian theory of psychology first, and understands and interprets astrology from within the Jungian framework. One of the things this does is to collapse the astrology symbols down so that they fit Jungian categories, and it is not always a good fit. We will see, with some of the astrologers we look at in the rest of this section, that each interprets the symbols in terms of their own framework and agenda.

Spiritual astrology assumes a metaphysical framework, and all of the planets and so on are interpreted as phases of the soul's journey to complete enlightenment. Isabel Hickey is squarely in the middle of the theosophical/new age/positive thinking current in the 20th century, and we will see that in her interpretations. She is also in the same current or thread as the later evolutionary and archetypal astrology.

Here is her description of the meaning of the glyph for Saturn. Note that giving the glyph itself a symbolic meaning is a distinctly theosophical development and likely goes back to Blavatsky.

> The symbol shows the cross of manifestation above the crescent; the Moon or personality held down by the cross. The only portion of ourselves that can be crucified is the dark self - the personality. Saturn can not touch YOU - only the mask which you wear. All restraints and limitations imposed by Saturn are really in the individual himself. The world of appearance is a mirror in which we see reflected our own nature.

This is carrying the Theosophical mix of Hindu theology with positive thinking to its logical and extreme conclusion. All the world is appearance created by the individual Self, so all the restrictions you experience are created by you. Note the distinctly Theosophical division into a dark and light self, a lower and higher self, where the lower self is illusion and selfish, while the higher self is real and selfless. Paradoxically, the real self is a selfless self, and you will have limitless freedom to express your real self when you are completely unselfish.

> Saturn is called the oldest of the gods and to this angel was given the rulership of the earth (the personality).

The personality is another name for the dark self or lower self.

> ...Saturn relentlessly brings back to the individual his own creation....It gathers the fruit of every experience and builds it into soul power. Saturn builds in time for eternity. In understanding the mission of Saturn lies the solution to the mystery of life. Saturn builds walls around the self until it is strong enough to stand without them. It is a constricting, contracting influence until the soul is strong enough to break down the selfishness and separateness in him and go free.

Again, you create your own reality, you harvest the results of your own thought. The limitations of Saturn are caused by selfishness and separateness. The purpose of the walls, the rules, the laws, is to eventually outgrow them. Get past those and it breaks all restrictions and you become limitless and free. Think very hard, and see if you can guess which planet represents breaking the walls and freedom.

This next quote is from a later section where a single key concept is given for each planet

> SATURN - THE TESTER
>
> Saturn's goal is **perfection**. Through the chastening process of testing, sorrow, delay, privation, man learns the purpose of life is not pleasure but to gain experience, patience, humility, wisdom and compassion....In Saturn's silence, in retrospection, meditation, concentration, looking within for guidance, and being willing to wait, Saturn helps us to bear our karma and pass the tests of life and finally enables us to reach the perfection we all must attain in the process of evolution.

Note the distinct mix of Darwin and evolution, western progress, Theosophy with Hindu thought and reincarnation, all mixing to make an endless process of progress and evolution towards perfection.

At this point in the book she also gives lists of basic, positive and negative traits of Saturn. All of them are psychological vices and virtues, qualities of personality. There is no mention of any meaning regarding anything outside of the human psyche.

There is some validity to the concepts that Hickey talks about here, and they tie in with Saturn's position at the border between time and eternity. In that sense, her spiritual perspective does connect up with some aspects of the traditional spectrum of Saturn's meaning. In later essays we will pick up and develop some of the themes she mentions.

Zipporah Dobyns

Zipporah Pottenger Dobyns (1921-2003) was a modern American astrologer. She was very interested in asteroids, and was involved in the development of the first asteroid ephemeris. Her son Mark Pottenger is well known for the American Ephemeris.

I am choosing to include Zipporah Dobyns in this survey since she is the astrologer who codified what she called the "12 Letter Alphabet", also known as the "Zip Code", where the signs, planets and houses are identical and interchangeable. The effect of this system on modern astrology is very broad and pervasive. Almost all modern astrologers, as soon as they think of the first house, immediately think Aries and Mars. It is partly due to her influence that you will see many if not most modern astrology books organized with sections combining Aries, Mars and the First House, then Taurus, Venus and the Second House, and so on. Traditional astrology does not make these connections and gives the planets, houses and signs each distinct sets of meaning. That association of sign, house and planet is a 20th century development, and people who move from modern to traditional astrology, like myself, often have a hard time breaking that automatic association.

In Dobyns' system, Saturn is associated with Capricorn, the one sign it rules in modern astrology. The next sign, Aquarius, is now given to Uranus for rulership, and that switch makes a profound difference in meaning both for the sign Aquarius and the planet Saturn.

As is typical of modern astrology, Dobyns associates each "Letter" of the 12 Letter Alphabet with a single core concept and principle. She derives the planet's meanings from that principle, and other associations with the planet tend to fall away. For Dobyns Saturn is the planet of Law, especially material law. We will see that the connotations of Law associated with Saturn in modern astrology have gotten thinner and more limited than in traditional astrology.

Here is her basic description of the planet's core meaning. Areas of emphasis are by Dobyns. Note that she speaks of 'The Saturn principle'

- Saturn is a core concept or principle now rather than a planet having a wide set of sometimes contradictory associations. Again, this is a very common and pervasive modern approach. Saturn has a role to play in her overall system, and the meanings of Saturn all come out of that role. The complexity of associations is gone.

> Based on our current state of understanding of the principles of astrology, Saturn (and its sign, Capricorn, and its 'natural' house in a horoscope - the tenth) are keys to the Law on all levels. They include **'natural laws'** like gravity and time which provide the framework in which we live in this material universe. The Saturn principle also includes **cultural regulations** such as stopping for red lights and going through green ones and driving the speed limit. It includes **authority figures** who enforce the law: parents, the police, the boss on the job...The Saturn principle also includes one's **conscience**, one's inner law, and guilt when we fail to live according to its limits. Plus it includes the consequences of how we have handled the laws in the past. In a nutshell, Saturn symbolizes **what we can do, what we can't do, and what we have to do if we want to survive in this material world**.

Now all of this is very good, and this indeed a very important part of Saturn's meaning. However, compared to our survey of traditional astrology, many other sorts of meanings have been lost - for instance, the association with cold damp places, with aging and death, with diseases like arthritis. None of those have any associations with the concept of Law, so they have been mostly dropped. Even the concept of Law associated with Saturn has become narrower and is limited to physical, cultural and material laws. The connection of Saturn with religious or moral or spiritual laws is unemphasized or lost.

Here I want to quote from her description of the meaning of letter 11 and Uranus, since it illustrates an interpretation that is very common in modern astrology and has no parallel in traditional astrology. This also impacts the meaning given to the planet Saturn.

Zipporah Dobyns

Letter eleven with Uranus, Aquarius, and the eleventh house shows the drive to go beyond the laws, to resist any limits. As an air side of life we may expand knowledge by inventing new technology. We may support democracy, equality, freedom, and human rights in general.

Saturn, Capricorn and the tenth house represent the laws that Uranus, Aquarius and the eleventh house now drive to go beyond. Here we have the opposition I talked about in the Old and New Cosmos chapter, of Saturn being the limitations that Uranus smashes through in the name of freedom. This is also the new and young replacing the old, and it plays into a world philosophy emphasizing freedom, growth, limitless expansion and progress. Saturn's meaning has gotten smaller, its range of associations is much thinner than in traditional astrology. The meanings attributed to Saturn here are good and valid, but much has been lost.

Liz Greene

Liz Greene, born in 1946, is a British Jungian psychologist and astrologer. Her books have been influential in the areas of modern humanistic and psychological astrology. Her viewpoint is that all of astrology, all of the symbolism of the planets, and actually all of human life, are to be viewed as being part of a psychological process. This all takes place inside the psyche, and external events only have meaning in so far as they reflect something going on in the psyche. The human consciousness is the measure of all things.

Greene's book, **Saturn: A New Look at an Old Devil**, is one of her best known works. The psychological setting is fully developed here in a new way compared to traditional astrology, and it does add a richness and flexibility of meaning in that one area. I will quote this at length and comment on it, since I think it clearly lays out many of the assumptions of modern humanistic and spiritual astrology, both in good ways and in limiting ways. The one area that I am going to be critical of Greene is where I think she unfairly caricatures and dismisses traditional astrology.

> In the tale of Beauty and the Beast, it seems somehow right, familiar, and fitting that the Beast, for all his ugliness, his sternness, and his capacity to inspire fear, should at the end turn into the Handsome Prince and marry the heroine...The Beast is always the dark face of the Handsome Prince.
>
> This kind of paradox seems to be an obvious facet of life... however, this quality of duality does not seem to have permeated our modern astrological viewpoint to any degree. There are still bad planets which are wholly bad and good planets which are wholly good...

I trust we have looked at enough traditional sources in our survey to show that last sentence is incorrect. It is true that you do see a lot of extreme descriptions in traditional astrology, but just as often you see mixes, contradictions, and all of the planets have a gamut of expressions from very positive to very negative. There are no planets that are either wholly bad or wholly good, in traditional or in modern astrology. Saturn is probably the most consistently negative in meaning of the traditional planets, yet we have seen that even with Saturn there are some very strong and positive features that are also mentioned through all the texts we looked at.

It is unfortunately very characteristic of modern astrology to paint a simplified caricature of traditional sources and then show how the modern viewpoint is superior. Again, this is part of our modern assumption of the inevitability of progress and evolution, that we are always moving forward, and the enlightenment of the present supersedes the darkness and superstition of the past. It is a blind spot of our modern world.

> Saturn symbolizes a psychic process as well as a quality or kind of experience. He is not merely representative of pain, restriction and discipline; he is also a symbol of the psychic process, natural to all human beings, by which an individual may utilize the experiences of pain, restriction, and discipline as a means of greater consciousness and fulfillment. Psychology has demonstrated that there is within the individual psyche a motive or impulsion towards wholeness or completeness.

This is a good insight, and this is one way of understanding Saturn. It also takes the modern psychological stance that the purpose of life is psychological wholeness.

> By his sign and house position Saturn denotes those areas of life in which the individual is likely to feel thwarted in his self-expression, where he is most likely to be frustrated or meet with difficulties.

Note the modern assumption that the purpose of human life is self-expression. This emphasis on the individual is a very recent development in human cultural history, an emphasis that is very characteristic of our modern world.

> In many instances Saturn seems to correspond with painful circumstances which appear not to be connected with any weakness or flaw on the part of the person himself but which merely 'happen', thereby earning the planet the title, 'Lord of Karma'."

Greene is merging two concepts into each other that I want to sort out and discuss separately.

Karma usually has the connotation of something happening to you because of some past actions, and that is very different from the idea of something just happening. That whole concept of things just happening we describe with the word Fortune, and that does seem to be a part of human experience. Much of modern astrology takes the stance that everything that happens to a person is their own fault, a concept which I find has some serious problems. The concept of Fortune has largely been lost. I think it has a useful place in astrology, and I will be examining Fortune further in a later section.

> This rather depressive evaluation remains attached to Saturn despite a most ancient and persistent teaching which tells us that he is the Dweller of the Threshold, the keeper of the keys to the gate, and that it is through him alone that we may achieve eventual freedom through self-understanding.

This Most Ancient and Persistent Teaching that she describes comes from the mid and late 1800's, the era of Theosophy. The term 'Dweller of the Threshold' was coined by the Victorian era novelist, Sir Edward Bulwer-Lytton, in a novel called **Zanoni**, a story of occult initiation, which was published in 1842. The term was later taken up into Theosophy and other occult writing from that era. It is characteristic of the sort of Theosophical spiritual and psychological model that provided the framework of understanding for much of modern astrology. I have not found any reference to Dweller of the Threshold prior to that.

Note here the assertion that the purpose of life is freedom, it is a psychological process, and it is achieved through self-understanding. This is characteristic of much modern astrology. This next piece is referring to the pain of Saturnian experiences.

> That there can be joy in this kind of experience is not so easily recognized; however, it is not enjoyment of pain which Saturn fosters, but rather the exhilaration of psychological freedom.

Again, the goal of life is freedom, psychological freedom. This next section is talking of how Saturnian experiences can be used.

> The ordinary answer to this question, when it is not the wholly useless reply of chance, is the equally useless idea that because these experiences represent the individual's karma, the present completion of an action or cycle begun in a past incarnation..."

This statement here is a good example of the unfortunate modern tendency to take traditional concepts and dismiss them without thoroughly understanding their meaning and usefulness. I will devote a later section of this book to showing how the 'wholly useless' concept of chance or fortune is actually very important. Discard it and you are left with a world where everything that happens to you is your own fault, an approach that can cause serious problems. I also think there is a place for the 'equally useless idea' of karma, and we will explore that later also.

> He does not consciously create these circumstances; it is the larger self, the total psyche, which is dynamic energy behind the individual's unfoldment.

The implication is that everything that happens to us is driven from within our own psyches, hence that we create our own reality, and thus everything that happens to us is our own creation and hence our own fault. For much of modern astrology the total psyche and the totality of the universe are implicitly identical.

> The majority of us are not yet at that stage where the dense molecules of matter move instantaneously at the bidding of our thoughts...

This is referring to the Theosophical claim of the existence of Ascended Masters, highly evolved human super beings, who have reached the point of evolution and enlightenment that the world instantly responds to their thought. This is very characteristic of the thinking of the late 1800s and early 1900s when much of the modern worldview of astrology took shape. In this model we all create our own reality, but we are evolving to the point where we can do it with full conscious control. The implication here is that the psychological freedom and wholeness we are evolving towards literally includes creating reality at the bidding of our thoughts and desires.

> Most people see their creations return to them as physical reality through indirect channels which appear to be someone else's fault...

Here she flat says that we all create our own reality from our psyches, from inside out. Because of lack of conscious awareness and control - because we are not yet highly evolved - it often involves negative events and suffering. When something bad happens to us we are seeing our own creations come back to us.

> And when responsibility is taken, it is usually colored black and called sin, which is an equally useless attitude.

I think this is another example of taking a traditional concept, caricaturing and dismissing it. She misunderstands the concept of human sin, and there is no place in her psychological model for any way it could be useful. I realize the concept of sin is out of favor these days, but there is valid insight in the idea of human sin that is worth considering. A concept of humanity that does not include sin runs the risk of hubris, inflating the power and value of the human psyche. There can be a very useful and humbling purpose in the awareness that I as a human being hold all the potential for evil inside me, and that sometimes my actions come out of that evil, whether I am aware of it or not, whether I control it or not.

> Usually all that is seen is the destructiveness. It has often been termed evil and given personification as an external energy or person known as Satan - who of course is very close to Saturn, complete with the hoofs and horns of Capricorn the Goat.

The identity of Saturn and Satan is very much a 20th century phenomenon, as is identifying Saturn with the sign Capricorn that it rules. In fact, a more common image for Saturn, the one that she has on the cover of her own book, is as Father Time. I cannot think of any traditional instances where the planet Saturn is pictured as the standard caricature of the Christian Devil, with horns and hoofs, tail, pitchfork and red tights. The goat is associated with the zodiac sign Capricorn, and in traditional astrology Capricorn and Saturn are not equated.

> The nature of this conflict between conscious and unconscious, dark and light, is neither good nor evil; it is necessary for growth because out of it comes eventual integration and greater consciousness.

Notice that this psychological model really has no place for moral evil. There is no evil, there is only unconsciousness, darkness. Dealing with evil involves the integration of opposites leading to expanded consciousness. The goal is psychological wholeness, awareness, and freedom. The implication seems to be that once we are whole, once there is no more unconscious darkness, that there will be no more evil.

There are some useful insights in Liz Greene's work. The psychological interpretation of the effect of Saturn does have validity, but as we have seen in the context of the overall tradition, it does not exhaust the meaning of Saturn. Useful as it is, I think the strictly psychological model here has some serious inadequacies and unbalances, that are very characteristic of our modern culture. A lot of the assumptions she makes here are common to our entire culture, and they are so much a part of the way we see the world that they are mostly invisible.

Steven Forrest - The Inner Sky

If you are a modern astrologer you have heard of Steven Forrest. His first book, **The Inner Sky**, first published in 1982, is one of the most popular introductory textbooks of astrology. Forrest has had a long career and has published many books, and through his school he has trained and influenced many modern astrologers.

His approach to astrology is very much a product of his times and is thoroughly modern, and thoroughly psychological. There is the implicit belief that all the cosmos, all the planets, are positive in effect, none are there to hurt. That is very much a 20th century judgment, and it ties into the strong positive thinking slant of our modern culture.

Note that this next quoted section is all emphasized in the original text.

> Function: The development of self-discipline. The development of self-respect. The development of faith in one's destiny. Making peace with solitude.
>
> Dysfunction: Depression, melancholy, cynicism, coldness, unresponsiveness, timeserving, drudgery, lack of imagination, suppression of emotions, materialism.
>
> Key Questions: In what area of life must I learn to act alone? Where will a lack of self-discipline lead most quickly to sorrow?

These attributions of Saturn are all solid and are similar to what we saw in traditional texts. Solitude and self-discipline are characteristic Saturnine strengths, and depression, melancholy and so on are characteristic weaknesses. Forrest frames the description in terms of how to use the strengths of Saturn to avoid having to experience the worst negative effects of the planet.

> Where will my ability to dream and have faith be most severely tested?

> When Retrograde: Deeply rooted self-sufficiency. May indicate a "loner". Enormous reserves of inner strength. Emotional self-discipline. May have a hard time saying "no".

A little later in the chapter on Saturn, after the listing of main attributes, we see this general description.

> Saturn - the old astrologers sometimes called it Satan. The Greater Malefic. Even now, the ringed planet is often viewed as the cosmic Frankenstein.

Repeating my earlier point, Saturn as Satan is a twentieth century attribution. Consider the phrase, 'Even now', which implies that even in our modern era we still make this old mistake. You would think that we would have grown past that by now. This assumes the belief in progress and that our new modern era is superior to previous ages. It also implies that, in earlier ages, the meanings of Saturn were entirely negative, and the term Malefic meant being only harmful.

> It is associated with depression and melancholia, with defeat, with loneliness and frustration. All that is true. It is an accurate description of the way Saturn manifests if we displease him. But that is not his purpose. No planet is there to hurt us.

The implication here is that Saturn only hurts us if we displease him. If we experience the wrath of Saturn it is our fault. This implies that, if we do things right and manage to please Saturn, that we will not experience those negative effects.

> Saturn teaches one virtue above all others: self-discipline. That is the key to understanding the symbol. Like Mars, the other so-called malefic, Saturn seeks to focus the will.
>
> To teach us that most elusive of arts: how to do exactly what we please.

Steven Forrest - The Inner Sky

I confess that this sentence took my breath away when I first read it. This sentence is an exact quote - the art of life is to do exactly what we please. We are here on earth to do whatever we want to do. That is very characteristic of late 20th century America, and especially of the period of the late 1970's and early 1980's when this book appeared. I am not aware of any previous historical cultures that would make that statement.

> How to make our **intentions** dominate over our fears, our laziness, our emotions.

> Saturn is often symbolized by the hermit, which is a very appropriate image. This is the planet of solitude. Wherever it lies in the birth chart, we find an area of life in which we must act alone. An area where self-sufficiency is everything. An area in which we can count on no one but ourselves. Even our rewards must be supplied by us alone.

In these quotes from Forrest there is an emphasis on the individual, and the importance and worth of the individual, that is without parallel in traditional astrology, but is characteristic of our modern era.

James Hillman and Archetypal Astrology

James Hillman (1926-2011) was a Jungian psychologist who eventually went his own direction and, to quote from the Wikipedia page, moved towards what is now called archetypal psychology. Hillman was not an astrologer himself, but he was very influential, and here he is talking about the meanings of Saturn as a psychological archetype. In this section I want to focus on how Hillman's approach vividly illustrates many of the assumptions of our modern world. The way he uses the meaning of Saturn here is characteristic of much of modern astrology.

This is from the introduction to the essay by Richard Tarnas p 11, talking about Hillman.

> "Hillman ...(is) using his insights into Saturn and the senex to reveal and subvert the orthodoxies he perceives as both structuring and constraining our cultural imagination.
>
> Hillman deftly deconstructs not just the field of psychology but the entire religious-philosophical meta-structure of Western civilization.
>
> He was always the fearless dissident, whatever the setting."

Notice the stance of rebellion. Deconstruct means destroy, tear down. Subvert has a similar connotation. The assumption here is that "the entire religious-philosophical meta-structure of Western civilization" needs to be criticized and destroyed. It is evil because it is constraining, limiting the imagination.

The assumption is that limits are evil, structure is evil. And the "fearless dissident" Hillman is taking on the task of rebelling against it. This is Uranus the rebel outside the ring of Saturn the constraining structure. Historically this stance of the "fearless dissident" is very popular and is a kind of modern norm, and being the fearless dissident has been popular since at least the late 1800's.

James Hillman and Archetypal Astrology

This is actually the language of heresy over against orthodoxy. Heresy is a technical religious term, and only really has meaning in the context of traditional Christianity. The shadow of the Christian church towers over this whole discussion with so much force that it is still being rebelled against over a century after Nietzsche proclaimed that God is dead. Hillman is a modern day brave Martin Luther nailing his 95 Theses to the church door. Archetypal astrology is in the form of a Protestant heresy - and note that the word Protestant just means Protester, and it is a characteristic stance of our culture.

There is a strong streak of modern culture that is in a stance of rebellion, of destroying old structure. In some ways we still live in a post-Christian world, a world in rebellion against that order. We live in a world of protest. The old structure is an evil to be deconstructed, subverted, torn down, destroyed - and Saturn is often used as a symbol for the old structure. The focus is on being over and against a structure to be destroyed. The new is not clearly defined, and I think that is intentional. The future is intentionally conceived as unformed, indefinite, open-ended. It is hinted at, implied, suggested, approached sideways.

This is freedom FROM restriction. This is the open-ended, formless world of the modern outer planets and infinite space past Saturn. It is the stance of Uranus, the planet just past Saturn, and we see that pairing of meanings repeatedly in modern astrology. If you want to talk of archetypes, I think of it as the stance of the rebellious child and teenager over against the elder parent and ancestors.

In this next section Hillman talks of senex and puer archetypes. In plain English, senex means very old person, and puer means child. In my comments I will use the plain equivalents rather than the Latin technical terms to clarify the meanings. The emphasis in this next paragraph is mine.

> "the main image of God in our culture: omniscient, omnipotent, seated and bearded, a ruler through abstract

principle of justice, morality and order...**The high God of our culture is a senex god**..."

Hillman is identifying the traditional structure of Western Judeo-Christian civilization, and all of the traditional structure of the traditional Christian God and world view, and summing it up by identifying it with the senex, a senile, old and dying man. Note that this is the first and only reference I have ever seen to Saturn as being omniscient and omnipotent. I think that reference is to the Christian God he is identifying with an old man here, rather than relating that to Saturn.

> "Because this archetype expresses all that is old, ordered and established, it has particular bearing upon our culture and its supposedly dead or dying God."

> "The breakdown of structure is the death of this particular structure, who is the Principle of Structure".

Now Saturn is identified with the breakdown of all structure, of the Principle of Structure itself. Structure is one of the core meanings of Saturn.

> "If the central fixation of our religious consciousness has aged into remote transcendence, there to wither and die, then the image in which we have been cast, reflecting this main god, is also passing away... The 'de-struction' of culture and the breakdowns in individual lives result from the transition of the senex dominant..."

> "What the Greeks called Kronos, and the Romans Saturn, our tradition has worshiped as 'Our Father which art in Heaven.' But gone from Heaven, and Heaven gone too, the senex now can be best encountered indirectly, through psychological phenomenology."

Traditional astrologers do not equate Saturn with the Christian father God image. I think he is saying that the structure of Western civilization is breaking down and dying, or may already be withered and dead. The Principle of Structure itself is collapsing. There are no fixed truths anymore, and all is change and flux.

Metaphorically Hillman is making an important point - we've smashed the house of the Father. The static order, the cathedral of the heavens, is gone, and the winds of chaos and change are blowing in from the outside. We are living in the ruins of a post-Christian world. I think he catches something very important about our modern world here.

That is the end of the quotes from Hillman. I want to talk about the change in worldview that Hillman is so vividly and clearly illustrating here.

The metaphoric stance of our culture has changed. The spire of the Gothic cathedral soaring up into the heavens has morphed into the Skyscraper, with a sort of magnificent stripped down rectangular plainness. The Gothic church aspires to God, the skyscraper is humanity ascending to the heavens, acknowledging nothing higher than itself, more like a tower of Babel.

Let's apply the Chesterton Test here. The word "destruction" is written as "de-struction" partly to illustrate it means to break down structure, and also because it defuses some of the concrete meaning and emotional charge of the word. It looks more abstract and less threatening than just using the word itself - something like, I didn't mean destruction, I meant de-struction. To Deconstruct a building sounds a lot less threatening than to destroy it.

If the Principle of Structure is withered and dead then what remains is open-ended lack of order, a potential for the new. If we really look at the evocative technical terms he uses, he seems to be saying that it is time for traditional western civilization to be destroyed, to collapse. De-structed, deconstructed, means torn down, ripped to pieces.

God is no longer in Heaven, and Heaven itself is gone. The Principle of Structure is gone. What we are left with, is images in the mind -

archetypes. And, these are images in the mind with no external referent or judging standard. It is open ended, it has potential, there is no fixed structure. Now that external Principle of Structure in the Universe has collapsed - or, in other words, now that God is dead - the only place to look for meaning, the only place where "the gods" still live, is within our minds. As with modern materialistic science, the external universe of matter is value-free, and has no inherent meaning other than what our minds impose on it.

There is a problem here with this model in explaining how astrology can be valid. If the gods exist only in our minds, then there is really no reason why there should be any correlation between the movement of physical bodies in the heavens around us, and anything at all of meaning in our lives. It cuts the ground out from under any meaning to astrology other than as personal projection. It also makes it very difficult to make sense of mundane or world astrology having any significance at all.

Hillman speaks of the high god of our culture as being a "senex god". Given that senex means old man or woman, if we live in a senex culture then it should be a culture in which senex values are highly honored and respected. This would mean that old age is honored and respected, and that the tradition of previous generations is respected and passed down.

I maintain that our current culture is the exact opposite of a senex culture. Our culture worships youth and not age, the new rather than the old. Far from being in brave rebellion against our current culture, I think Hillman is very typical of it.

We are in a culture that worships youth, that worships the new, that dismisses and denigrates the old, and that believes in perpetual progress. Much of our current culture is in a general stance of youthful rebellion over against a tradition that is perceived as outmoded, repressive, structured, withering and dying. The general stance of our culture values freedom, and it is freedom FROM all restriction, a movement towards limitless expansion. It is a breakdown of all restriction to expand metaphorically into limitless outer space, or limitless inner psychological space.

As a final note to this chapter - I am finishing up this book in September 2019. As I write this, there are a couple of very prominent examples in the news of young children being spokespeople, or authorities, or bearers of important messages. There are some examples of children gathering as groups in demonstrations and rallies, and there are a few young people being given prominent front page news coverage to have their say on current issues. The unspoken assumption is that we are supposed to listen to them precisely because they are children. They are the future, they are the new authorities, so their voice weighs far heavier than that of old people, whose time is past and should now step aside and let the young take over.

We do not live in a senex culture; quite the opposite. We live in a culture that worships the young and the new, and devalues the old and outmoded and old fashioned. The brave young rebels are the new normal, and the heretics and protesters are the new orthodoxy.

Current Archetypal Astrology

The quotes here are from a contemporary book by Renn Butler named, **Pathways to Wholeness: Archetypal Astrology and the Transpersonal Journey**. He is working in a model called Transpersonal Psychology which integrates Jungian archetypes with exploration into "non-ordinary states of mind", mystical states of oneness. He is building on the work of people like Stanislaus Grof, and unstated and uncredited in the background is the specter of Timothy Leary, the explorer of inner space from the Sixties.

This book is very explicit about the overall cosmology, and it is basically the same set of assumptions we see from Dane Rudhyar and Theosophy, through Liz Greene and Jungian astrology, to our more recent Evolutionary astrology.

> In the realm of perception, Saturn manifests through the *hylotropic* or "moving toward matter" mode of awareness - the natural complement to the *holotropic* or "moving toward wholeness" principle.

Since wholeness is defined as the good, the ultimate goal of the process, then Saturn is by definition the exact opposite.

> In order to create the physical universe, the Absolute Consciousness splits off parts of itself into separate, distinct entities in time and space...As the Absolute incarnates and subdivides into more and more diverse entities a process of separation and self-forgetting occurs.

> Saturn represents this dividing and separating principle. It is the force of contraction that causes the many separate units of awareness in the material world to forget who they really are. Every form in the universe, whether an archetype, an inanimate object, or a living being was once, and still is, a part of this greater cosmic field - which is why

Current Archetypal Astrology

> the spiritual journey is often referred to as *awakening* or *Self-realization*...

Notice that archetype is listed as a "unit of awareness", which I think means a conscious living being. The term archetype effectively means what used to be called a god, an angel, or a demon. The old cosmos has been replaced with the subjective cosmos of astrology - and yet he is strongly implying here that archetypes have some kind of conscious existence in their own right. Instead of Angels in the mind of God, we have Archetypes in the field of Absolute Consciousness.

The emphasis in this next section of quotes is mine, as it sums up a lot of modern astrology.

> The process of incarnation is so painful that we forget where we came from, and the highest yearning of our soul is to regain this lost wholeness and remember who we really are. **This awakening process is symbolized in different ways by the archetypes Uranus, Neptune, and Pluto.**

> The solar systems exists as a map of the human awakening process. Our personal human psychology is writ large in the heavens. When you think of it, this is a very human-centered form of cosmology, and it projects our human conscious evolution out into the shape of the heavens. Instead of humanity being created in the image of God, we have the cosmos created in the image of human psychological process.

The cosmos exists in the image of the human psyche. We project ourselves out into the heavens. Human consciousness expands to infinity and engulfs the entire cosmos.

> A well-integrated Saturn principle confers in people feelings of responsibility, humility, and patience. They will live comfortably within nature's material boundaries while recognizing that consciousness itself is without

> boundaries…[Saturn's] lessons help people to cultivate the discipline, endurance, and fortitude that can ultimately liberate them from Saturn's unconscious oppression over the human mind.

Again we have that characteristically modern language, talking of liberation from oppression by getting past restricting structures. The final goal is a realization of consciousness without boundaries. Any sort of structure or boundary is a source of unconscious oppression, it hems in our minds. I think this series of quotes clearly spells out a lot of the assumptions behind much of modern astrology.

Uranian Astrology & its Descendants

I'm going to group three astrologers together here who share a common heritage and approach. All heavily emphasize mathematics, geometry and aspects, and all emphasize the scientific and predictive side of astrology.

Also, each of these astrologers has distilled each of the planets down to a core concept or principle, and the interpretation comes from how these principles combine. The elemental qualities are not used, nor are sign rulerships, nor are any mythical qualities. The interpretations are mostly concrete, specific events and people. All of these systems of meaning work very well with realistic chart reading, and they are well worth learning and pondering. While they lack the broad range of concrete associations of the traditional correspondence lists, they have a kind of elegance that can generate specific meanings by context. I know from experience that all of these systems work very well.

This kind of approach to the meanings of planets, giving a few core concepts, along with key words and principles, has become very popular in modern astrology. What marks the Uranian school, and their followers, is that they tend to be solid, concrete, specific, and are not as vague or psychologically suggestive as keyword lists by humanistic or psychological astrologers.

Alfred Witte - Uranian Astrology

Uranian astrology, the earliest school of the three, arose in Germany in the 1920's. Witte is the genius who came up with working with charts on dials, especially the 90 degree dial, as a way to easily focus in on important hard aspects.

His main reference textbook, **Rules for Planetary Pictures**, combines the meanings of the planets in twos and threes with each other based on geometric configurations.

I am here giving an excerpt of his meanings of Saturn. First he gives a stand-alone definition, and then details how Saturn combines with the other traditional planets. Witte takes these pairs and then shows how they in turn combine with a third planet or point. I am keeping his abbreviations of the planet and point names as they are a characteristic part of his style.

> Saturn - Restriction. To bridle. To hinder. Separations. Losses.
>
> Sat - Asc - To be separated from other people. Estrangement. To experience refusal. Given the cold shoulder.
>
> Sat - MC - To slow down or hinder others. To feel deserted. To feel a burden. To take over a duty. Obligations. Depression, inhibition.
>
> Sat - Sun - To take leave. Bodily separations. Old man and old age. The serious man. Personal and physical hindrances and difficulties.
>
> Sat - Moon - Self-reserve. To avoid women. Discontented. To be separated from the public. Restrain, separate. Despair. Depressed mind. Old, single, separated or unhappy woman. Widow. The hours one has to be alone. Evening hours.
>
> Sat - Merc - Thoughts of separation. Travels. Logic. Philosophical thinking. Competence to form an opinion, to pass judgment. To ponder. Deliberation.
>
> Sat - Ven - Separation of love. Interrupted harmony. Hindered inclinations. Passing affection. Love's sorrow. Illegitimate birth.
>
> Sat - Mars - Obsequies (Funeral services). Funeral. Periodic work. (Mars as labor, work.) Interruption of work. Sicknesses. Action of Separation. Death.

Sat - Jup - To have no luck. Money losses. Losses of real estate. "Ripe old age." Inconstant success. Successful separation. Separated from luck. Buildings. Changes of residence.

Reinhold Ebertin - Cosmobiology

Ebertin, also German, was originally a colleague of Witte's who went off and formed his own system, which is a kind of streamlined version of Uranian, keeping the emphasis on aspects and dial work. Ebertin also worked heavily with midpoints as places where the energies of planets combined. His book, **The Combination of Stellar Influences**, is his main reference work and has been widely influential. It is one of my personal favorite astrology texts, and I find its meanings and combinations to be very useful, logical and suggestive.

As in the Witte's Uranian textbook, Ebertin looks at the planets in pairs, and then gives tables of how those pairs would interact with a third planet. I will give the main definitions of Saturn by itself, then an example of Saturn plus the planet Mercury. The plus and minus signs (+ and -) are used by Ebertin meaning positive and negative interpretations, with the C meaning somewhere in between.

Saturn

Principle - inhibition, concentration.

Psychological Correspondence

+ Concentration, consolidation, perseverance, seriousness, the ability to learn from experience, economy.

- Inhibition, melancholy, reserved and taciturn, increasing loneliness, isolation, eccentration, distrust, stinginess, lack of adaptability.

Biological Correspondence - The bony structure, the process of hardening up, stone formation, the loss of organs, old age.

Sociological Correspondence - Hard working, inhibited or sad people. Agriculture, mining, real estate.

Mercury/Saturn

Principle - Depth of thought, mental work.

+ Logical thinking, thoroughness, concentration, ability to come straight to the point, love of tidiness, ability to organize, industrious, the application of method, philosophical thinking.

- An inhibited mental development (caused sometimes by defective speech), distrust. Shy, narrow-minded, conservative attitude, self-willed or obstinate, an uncommunicative and reserved disposition.

C Obstinate, tenacity or endurance, clumsiness or heaviness, industrious, the state of enduring or suffering without yielding.

Biological Correspondence

Blocking of the nervous system, pain-conducting nerves. The functional relationship of the nervous system to the organs of speech and hearing.

Probable Manifestations

+ A slow but sure advancement in life, opportunities to gain experience, ability to concentrate deeply on philosophical problems, opportunity to travel.

- Hard times during infancy and adolescence, a difficult and laborious rise in life, estrangements, frequent separations.

David Cochrane - Vibrational Astrology

David Cochrane is active and at the peak of his influence today - I am writing this in 2019. His system of vibrational astrology views the planets and their interactions as energy patterns that manifest in characteristic ways. He is building on the work of John Addey and Harmonic Astrology, which examines aspects formed by dividing up the chart wheel by different numbers or harmonics, with each number having its own characteristic meaning and expression. For meanings, Cochrane emphasizes the various harmonics as giving the meanings, so the planets have most meaning in terms of their harmonic or vibrational interaction.

Cochrane's work is another good example of taking a planet's associations and distilling it down to a core concept or principle that works out very well in practice. Again, it lacks some of the concrete richness, variation and untidiness of the traditional lists, but it is elegant, streamlined and functional. The complexity and richness of meaning in Harmonic astrology and in Cochrane's vibrational astrology comes from the meanings of the aspects based on different numeric divisions of the chart wheel. The planet symbolism is fairly straightforward and simplified, and the aspect and number symbolism is highly developed.

This is the section on the core meaning of Saturn in Cochrane's first book.

> Saturn
>
> Like Jupiter, there are many associations with Saturn, a few of which are: detachment, rigidity, maturity, wisdom responsibility, frustration, inhibition, isolation, separation, failure, death, dryness, heaviness, and authority.

> I view Saturn as a drive to remove excess, fat, and anything frivolous, while preserving what is essential. Saturn tends to remove extravagances and sometimes even simple pleasures and focus our attention on our responsibilities. Saturn dislikes extravagances and distractions. Saturn values what is essential and important, and casts everything else aside. Virtually all of the traditional associations of Saturn can be viewed as manifestations or consequences of Saturn's focus on what is essential.

A couple of points to note here. First, I think what Cochrane means by the traditional associations is the list in the first paragraph above - and notice that they are all abstract concepts - there are no plants, or land near water, or specific diseases like arthritis. I think the core point that he makes is indeed very useful, but for me as a traditional astrologer I think it omits many dimensions of meaning.

Notice also that Cochrane's system does not place the bulk of its interpretation on the planets, or the signs and houses. Like harmonic astrologers, Cochrane's system places the main focus of its interpretation on specific numbers and aspects, divisions of the circle by whole numbers with specific meanings. Complexity in one part of the system is balanced by a simplifying of other parts of the symbolism.

The Contribution of Modern Astrology

The first couple of times that I looked over the material in this historical survey, the main thing that struck me in the modern writing is the shift of meaning, from external and factual to internal and psychological. I was also struck by how the meanings had gotten thinner and lost some of their rich detail. That is a very important and even dominant part of modern astrology.

However, there is another very important and vital development that I did not immediately spot, because it has been so much a part of my astrology world I take it for granted. There is a vital and wonderful new development here. Modern astrology definitions of Saturn and the other planets are about the PURPOSE that the planet serves, what it is created to accomplish.

Not the WHAT, but the WHY.

The descriptions of Saturn and other planets are all ways of addressing questions of meaning, value and significance. To my knowledge this really is a new development. I cannot think of where that question is addressed anywhere in the traditional literature, which is exclusively focused on WHAT will happen. Go back and read over the historical descriptions and you will see the new element quietly appear in pretty much all the modern writing. Even the psychological analysis which is present in traditional astrology, describes character traits, how they express, and not what their purpose is.

Addresses a Modern Need for Meaning

This new dimension of modern astrology addresses the particularly 20th century existential dilemma. We are faced with a meaningless universe and we need to have a way of making sense of our lives, and astrology can help with that. In terms of my own practice I find that the needs of the people I work with weigh heavily on the *why* part of the spectrum. My clients in general are often at least as interested in the question of *making sense* of what they are going through as they are in wanting to know what will happen.

The insights of the modern astrologers I quoted are excellent examples of how to make sense of the meaning of Saturn, what might be the purpose of Saturn related events. For instance, consider Saturn as serving the function of a tester, as representing the law, as showing us the consequences of our actions, and the need to take responsibility. Part of Saturn's effect can be interpreted as trimming excess fat, as David Cochrane said.

All of these are valid ways to interpret Saturn that I think we can argue may have been implicit in the traditional material but are only made explicit here in the modern work. These interpretations are valid, they are new, and they are developing new dimensions of the meanings of Saturn and of all the other planets.

We focused mainly on astrologers with a psychological emphasis, but we see the same new development with the efforts of the math and geometry focused astrologers - Witte, Ebertin, David Cochrane. What these people are doing is trying to think the planets back to core principles, and their insights contribute an enormous amount. In their case the great weight of the interpretive symbolism arises from the math and geometry, so the abstract but flexible core principles serve well in their systems.

The Role of Myth

This dimension of meaning is also a place where the modern work with myths has a special contribution to make. I am thinking particularly of the work of Steven Forrest here. From everything I have read by him, and heard of how he does readings, his particular strength is in providing stories, metaphors that people can use to make sense of what is happening to them and to find a sense of meaning and purpose to the events.

The Contribution of Modern Astrology

I think this is where his past life work has a valid place. Traditional astrologers who criticize him for saying he claims to tell people their past lives are missing the point, and are not fairly describing what he actually does. What he is offering is stories, metaphors, patterns that help people see the meaning and purpose of what they are going through.

I think this is important to get clear. The modern emphasis in some astrology on past life work makes no sense in terms of traditional prediction since by definition it cannot be verified. However, past life work *as metaphor*, as pattern for giving a life a sense of purpose, of meaning, of direction, is very useful and valuable. This is working at a whole different task than traditional astrology, and I suspect it is this difference that accounts for some of the misunderstandings going both ways between traditional and modern astrologers. They are doing different things.

This also clarifies something important about the purpose of myth. I find that myth does not work well for strictly predictive work. For instance, I find it to be very misleading when it is used for something like predicting the outcome of a political election. Myths are flexible and formless enough that they lend themselves to wish fulfillment, and the odds that the astrologer will predict an outcome that aligns with their desires is very high. Myth and story work poorly for predictive work, but they do serve a very important purpose in answering questions of meaning. For that they excel.

In this case it is helpful to understand both what these different approaches to astrology are in traditional and modern, and how they each have valid applications, they each have their strengths and weaknesses.

Emphasis on Free Will and Choice

Another contribution that modern makes is the emphasis on how human free will, choice and action contribute to the result. I personally think it is over-emphasized and needs to be balanced with a world where we often have little or no control, but it is indeed an important part of human life. Traditional texts are phrased in terms of what will happen to a person. They are not phrased in terms of offering choices and potentials - that is a characteristically modern development. The emphasis on the chart as potential to be fulfilled is also modern.

Focus on the Individual

This new focus on meaning connects with the distinctly modern emphasis on the importance of the individual human life. In the traditional world it is assumed that human life is part of a larger order which is a given. Traditional astrology shows how that life works out within that larger context, but it doesn't really consider the question of each human life having its own purpose and meaning.

In the traditional context, if you were born a slave or a king, destined for hardship and disease or wealth and power, that was your lot in life. The whole question of fairness or meaning or purpose for the individual just doesn't come up in the same way. You could describe the traditional cosmos as showing the will of God or the gods, and the pattern of purpose is in the collective, the cosmos as a whole.

I personally think we are best served by considering both aspects of human experience, the human as individual, and the human as part of a larger whole.

Meaning and Context

Questions of meaning are related to context, and here there is a huge difference between traditional and modern. Modern human life lacks a context. We are dealing with that yawning chasm between inner and outer reality, and to have any sense of meaning we need a context.

In the traditional cosmos the context is there. There is a seamless connection between inner and outer all held together by god or the gods. There is an overall pattern, and inner and outer are part of the same inter-woven pattern. Our modern exclusive emphasis on the importance of the isolated individual life is unthinkable in the traditional cosmos. Again, the traditional cosmos is so very different from our modern assumptions that it is very hard for us to grasp.

Part of what I wish to show in the next section of this book is a way that we can think of our lives as still having a meaningful context and connection with the greater universe we inhabit.

Summing Up

I think we have shown that the worlds of traditional and modern astrology each have something very valuable to bring to the table, and that our astrological world will be richer as we acknowledge and include the best of both.

In the remainder of the book I will address some dimensions of the meaning of Saturn that I think need emphasis in the modern world. I also want to address the issue of the overall context and coherence of the world, how we can take different take on the traditional world to close the inner/outer gap in the modern world, and re-establish a sense of overall order and law.

Part Two: The Eternal Law

Introduction

The full meaning of Saturn in the traditional cosmos includes some important dimensions that I think have either fallen out of modern astrology or are under-emphasized. The traditional meanings of Saturn group into a few main areas, and will examine one particular meaning here.

Perhaps the most important and distinctive group of meanings comes from Saturn's being on the boundary of the temporal and eternal worlds. That meaning only makes sense if we can still conceive of an eternal world with unchanging laws in a way that makes sense in our modern world.

The essays in this section make the case that the idea of eternal law is alive, vibrant and useful today. I am describing how I as a traditional astrologer look out at the world today, and sharing the kinds of thought processes making eternal law a living concept for me.

I look to traditional sources for the main concepts I present here. Most appropriately I am drawing on Greece, the birthplace of western astrology, and the philosophical framework of Plato and other members of the Platonic tradition. This framework has had a powerful formative influence on our Western culture, and it has been a living part of our world throughout the entire period of traditional astrology, from the Hellenistic era, through the Catholic philosophical synthesis of Thomas Aquinas in the Middle Ages, right up to the world of William Lilly in the seventeenth century.

Platonic Model of the Universe

Astrology today does not have a coherent place in our modern worldview. it is a floating system with no roots and no supporting logic, and we have no coherent theory to explain why it works. That is not the case in the traditional world. In the traditional model the world of astrology is part of an overall way of thinking about and structuring the entire universe.

We will use the Platonic tradition to provide a context for understanding astrology today, sketch out the basics of the Platonic model, and show where Saturn fits in that model. I draw on the entire Platonic tradition, especially the extensive writings of the late Platonist Proclus, who created an elaborate metaphysical and theological system in which the gods served specific functions in the overall structure.

This is a very brief and simplified overview of a complex and beautiful system. I am laying out the main outlines to paint a picture, and make the shape of the whole visible.

The Platonic Model

A good metaphor that illustrates the Platonic world is to think of the source of all as a universal Mind, a Mind that creates in structures and patterns. The universe is created in stages or levels, starting at the source at the top with the universal Mind and working downwards, with our changeable material universe being at the bottom. The process works from the most abstract down to the most concrete.

Structural Elements - The Forms

The framework of the universe, the structural elements, are what Plato called the Ideas or the Forms. These are abstract patterns, laws that hold all of creation together.

Platonic Model of the Universe

Gregory Bateson defined God as, The Pattern That Connects. That is a very good metaphor for the overall system of the Platonic Ideas.

Our minds do not create these ideas. It would be more accurate to say that these ideas create our minds. The thoughts we think are images or reflections of these eternally existing Forms. We see the structure of the universe mirrored in our minds.

The structure of our minds and the structure of reality follow the same model, and it is all a coherent ordered whole, a system.

This is very different from a modern scientific concept of a material World Out There separate from us, with our minds In Here trying to connect to it. In the Platonic model the same Mind that creates the external world also creates our minds, and the inner and outer patterns are connected. This does not mean that our mental models perfectly match the eternal Forms, but it does mean that our models are not arbitrary. They have a base or source in the actual structure of the Universe. The closer our thoughts come to the real structure of the universe, the clearer they are, and the more powerful they are.

The Forms are the Gods

These Forms, these structural patterns, are alive. They are created by the universal Mind and they share the life of that mind. They are patterns that are themselves intelligent and creative. The Platonic forms are ideas, and they are also very close to what we can call gods in the Greek polytheistic sense. The One God of monotheist religions like Christianity might better be thought of as related to the source from which the gods, the Forms, the ideas emerge. I like the Platonic metaphor of the source of all as the One and the Good, beyond anything we conceive, underlying all things and holding all things together.

> **The Pattern that Connects is Alive, and the structural elements that hold it all together are also alive.**

Great Chain of Being

In the modern world, if we think of God at all, it is likely to be as some sort of distantly removed transcendent being who exists Up There Somewhere, like the bad tempered Old Man that Hillman talked about. God is up there and we are down here, and there is no real living connection between us. That concept is a side effect of the change in the concept of God that began with the Protestant revolution and was developed further in the birth of the modern scientific worldview.

In the traditional model you have God or the source of all up at the top of a hierarchy or chain, with we humans on earth down at the bottom, and in between are a whole series of intelligent entities forming a connection, a bridge from the highest to the lowest. The whole system is connected. Platonism conceived that order as a series of higher and lower gods, with the lower gods being called daemons. The daemons are lower level intelligences that serve to connect the human soul with the higher levels.

God connects to the Gods, which in turn connect to the lower level gods we call Daemons, which then in turn connect to the human Soul. The whole system is a living circuit, called the Great Chain of Being. That Great Chain connects every created entity at any level, through a series of graduated steps, all the way back to the Source.

The traditional Christian church kept that model, putting the father God at the top, and they kept and renamed the intermediary beings as principalities, powers, archangels, angels and so on. It is the same great chain described with other terms.

With the Protestant revolution all of those intermediate beings were viewed as superstitions and were swept aside. This effectively destroyed any coherent connection between the Source of all and the material world we inhabit. We had a ladder from earth leading up to heaven, and the ladder was kicked aside. Once the intermediate connection was removed, sooner or later the whole conceptual system was bound to fall apart, and in our modern world we are left with the ruins.

But the Living System, the Pattern that Connects, is still there. God, and the gods, by whatever name, are still alive, and still form the basis of our world. The Order is still there, and we can still connect up with that Order, both in our minds and in the world around us. The fine art of astrology is part of how we can do that.

Eternal and Changing Worlds

Working from the top down, the Source of all is prior to change, prior to space and time. We live in the world of space and time, a world of constant change. If you have the unchanging world up there, and the changing world down here, we need a way of connecting the two.

In the traditional model of the cosmos, the bridge or connection between eternity and time is formed by the orbits of the traditional planets in astrology.

Down here is what is traditionally called the sublunary world, the world inside the Moon's orbit, which is the world of the four elements, of physical matter as we know it. Inside that lunar orbit everything is a mutable and somewhat disordered mess. We can predict the movements of the planets with hundreds of years ahead with great accuracy, but we can't count on accurately predicting the weather a day ahead.

The traditional planets, from Mercury on up to Saturn, serve as part of the Great Chain, the bridge connecting the eternal order up there with the changing order down here. The planets exist in what was thought of as an intermediate world between eternal and temporal. The planets all move, but their movement is very ordered, very predictable. Conceptually they are somewhere between changeable and unchangeable, and they have a predictable and everlasting order. **We still count on the amazing predictability of that order every time we cast an astrology chart.**

Platonic Model of the Universe

Saturn holds a special place in this model. **Saturn is at the border between the Eternal and the Temporal worlds, reflecting the eternal order down into the world of time.**

Unchanging and Changing Levels of Mind

The unchanging and changing levels of the universe are mirrored in different levels of our minds and souls. Our minds don't work in such a way that we can think of everything all at once. Like the changing world around us, we need to think our way through things a step at a time.

To learn a new skill you first have to learn all the individual elements one by one, and then gradually connect them. If you persevere, you get to a point where the whole thing comes together, and you can see the entire pattern of the system all at once. The Platonic name for that kind of all-at-once knowing is Intellect. I call it as Unitive Thought, seeing the whole pattern all at once.

Just as the eternal and unchanging world is mirrored in our changing world, so the eternal and unchanging order of Intellect is mirrored in our minds in the process of Reason. Reason is what makes us distinctive human; it is our ability to think, to connect, to compare and judge. This sets us apart from all other animals, and from any other living being.

In my mind I sum up this essay you are reading in two words, Eternal Law. That is Intellect. It is taking me pages and pages trying to explain what I mean by those words so that you can grasp them also, and that is Reason. This entire chapter is devoted to building up a coherent model of the world. The whole model all at once is Intellect. The process we're going through to be able to grasp that model is Reason.

The source creates from the top down all at once - that is Intellect. We have to learn things from the bottom up, one piece at a time - that is Reason.

Platonic Model of the Universe

In the Platonic model Saturn reflects the unchanging order of Intellect into our minds and into the created Universe. It gives us an unchanging standard to measure and judge by. It also shows us that order unfolding over time, and the consequences of that unfolding. Saturn bridges Eternity and Time.

Saturn, Jupiter and Creation

Plato's creation myth is laid out in the Timaeus, a very complicated and cryptic dialog filled with intricate mathematical and astrological symbolism. According to the Timaeus our world was not created directly by The Source of All. The task of creation was assigned to the Demiurge, a creator or craftsman god given the task of building the manifest universe on the model of pre-existing eternal laws, patterns, forms. In Greek mythology the Demiurge is Zeus, or Jupiter in the Roman pantheon. The planet Jupiter in astrology is a lower level reflection of that same world-building function.

In the act of creation Zeus looked up to eternal patterns for models. The source of those patterns is Kronus, or Saturn in the Roman pantheon. Saturn reflects the unchanging patterns to Jupiter to be used as structural guidelines. In mythical language, Saturn is the father of Jupiter.

The planet Saturn is a lower level reflection of Eternal Law or Intellect being mirrored down into the temporal world through the Demiurge Zeus or Jupiter.

Eternal Law

Since the era of traditional astrology we have experienced a change in our conception of the cosmos; there is no denying that. We no longer look out and see an unchanging, immobile sphere, and we likely never will again. That model no longer matches our modern science, and we will never completely return to the world of traditional astrology.

I want to consider how we in our modern world can best understand the unchangeable, reliable and eternal law structuring the cosmos we experience. As astrologers we can can think about the laws of mathematics, geometry and astronomy that we use to calculate our planetary positions, and that underlay all our astrology tools.

In order to practice astrology you either have to use the necessary calculations, and reference material like ephemerides and tables of houses, or you need access to a person or machine that does the calculations for you. Given those tools you can draw up a horoscope chart for any date, time and place, for hundreds of years into the past or future, and calculate the planetary and house positions of that chart to an accuracy of a fraction of a degree of error, far less than 1% error. That is an astoundingly reliable and consistent system. These calculations have worked for thousands of years, and we have every reason to think they will continue to work, and no reason for thinking they will one day stop working. Even if we mentally project into an unimaginably far future where our solar system falls apart, we have no reason to think that the laws of mathematics we have been using to calculate with will fail to be valid.

Is the mathematics that we use for our astrology perfect? No. The tables we use of planetary positions use what is referred to as Ephemeris Time, which cannot take into account the very small amount of variation in the exact length of a solar year. That variance, called Delta T, cannot be calculated in advance, and it ends up being anything from a few seconds to a few minutes per year. This is an infinitesimally small percentage of variance.

Eternal Law

This is a very complex, robust and reliable calculation system that corresponds to the position and motion of physical bodies in the heavens. It is not just abstract, and not just in our minds; it corresponds to external world conditions that are empirically verifiable. That is what I mean by a structural principle wired into the inner fabric of the universe. Those underlying principles or mathematics, geometry and astronomy give us a window into how we can understand the real world of the Platonic forms or ideas.

It is also worth considering the astounding regularity of the daily revolution of the earth on its axis, and the yearly revolution of the earth around the Sun. Again, it is not perfectly regular, and there are very minor differences in the length of each day, but for all intents and purposes it is a fixed, unchanging, very predictable and reliable order. If you have a table of houses, which is a mathematical construct based on the daily rotation of the earth, you can draw up the houses for any chart at any point in time we can conceive, past or future. Stop for a minute and let that really sink in; since it is so very familiar it is easy to miss seeing how very wondrous that is.

I maintain that it is very, very reasonable to argue that our mathematics and geometry are pointing at and mirroring underlying eternal laws of mathematics that are an inherent part of the structure of the Universe itself. Those laws are not just in our minds; they mirror something real, empirical and measurable.

Regardless of what happens in the history of the universe, regardless of what changes happen, what planets and stars come and go, 2 + 3 will still equal 5, and the 3 angles of a triangle on a flat plane will always add up to 180 degrees. Here I am referring to traditional Euclidean geometry, which still has extremely good predictive and measuring power after thousands of years of use, but even given the fact that there are now non-Euclidean geometries that can be used to make scientifically useful models, I maintain that this points to a higher level mathematical order. If there were not such an inherent order the mathematical calculations would have no validity, consistency or predictive power.

Eternal Law

In the modern world we tend to think of our minds as imposing order and value out onto the world, and some modern scientists maintain that science consists only of mental models that have no real correspondence with any reality. Stating that more bluntly, our minds invent these scientific rules, and we use them because they happen to work. I argue that it makes much more sense to say that our minds perceive and mirror valid structural principles of the universe itself. Without those structural principles any models we build would be arbitrary, and there would be no grounds for preferring any one to another.

Granted that we are mirroring an eternal order in our temporal experience, the mirror's shape is not arbitrary. Our mental model points to an order that is actually there, that exists independent of any human mind that perceives, calculates and validates it.

It is worth emphasizing that this system is not static, it is a form and shape that unfolds over time. It mirrors the Saturnian principle that we can only get at the full eternal order, the order outside of and prior to space and time, by considering full completed cycles within time. It is the difference between tracing a circle with a pencil on paper, which illustrates time, and then seeing the circle all at once, which illustrates eternity.

That is also why old age, the years associated with Saturn, are the years that it is appropriate to be returning to contemplate these eternal forms. In the later years we have had enough life experience to get a sense of full cycles, of full lifespans, of people and performers and businesses and countries being born, growing, flourishing, falling apart and dying, to be succeeded by other forms.

It feels appropriate that in our modern world we need to take movement in time into account to get a sense of eternal order.

Astrology and her sister disciplines, mathematics, geometry and astronomy, are among the best of subjects to study to get a sense of the order and wonder of the universe. Astrology at its highest is a form of contemplative discipline, and studying mathematics, geometry and astrology is the closest we can come to communing with the mind of God. It restores the sense of primitive wonder at the amazing living structure of this weird and wonderful world we live in.

More on the Platonic Forms

In text books about Platonic astrology you will sometimes see the Platonic forms explained something like this: for every living horse in the world, there is an eternal Platonic form or idea of a horse which serves as the model for that animal. This example makes the Forms seem something like a big template library or a box of cookie cutters with pre-planned shapes. I don't think that is what the original concept of the Forms means.

I find it more useful to think of the Forms as structural principles or design principles, and the most abstract and inclusive principles are the most powerful of all and can generate more related forms. For instance, a geometric triangle is an example of a form; it has a strict definition and set of characteristics, and you can generate an infinite number of physical triangles of all shapes, sizes and variants without in any way depleting the original form.

The science of Geometry is a more inclusive, higher level form. We can include both Euclidean and non-Euclidean geometries, each of which starting with different postulates. Rather than negating the Platonic notion of forms, I think those two systems of geometry are part of a higher level Form that is a kind of meta-geometry which can generate multiple systems, all of which have shared characteristics, and all of which point to structural principles of the universe. Mathematics in general is another good example of a high level form, a structural principle.

There is something distinctive and important about the Platonic approach to studying these structural principles. Unlike our modern approach to sciences like mathematics and geometry, the Platonic disciplines are to be studied for their own sake and for the light they throw on the structure of the mind of the Source. For the Platonists, what they call Theoretical Arithmetic is a higher discipline than Practical Arithmetic.

In the Platonic system these numbers intersect with the living world of values, and the world of the gods. As an example of how that was presented, the late Platonist Proclus wrote a book on the Elements of Theology that is modeled on the geometric postulates and theorems of Euclid, and he also wrote a philosophical and theological commentary on Euclid. Science, philosophy and theology are all part of a larger seamless system of the science of the structure of the universe.

To really begin to understand how rich this concept of the Forms or Ideas really is, you need to combine theoretical or scientific concepts with basic moral structural concepts like Justice, and then combine those with the idea of these forms being living Gods, so that the forms themselves are conscious and creative. Put these concepts together and you are beginning to touch the hem of the living divine world of conscious light which the forms express.

This is why Plato and other members of the Platonic and Pythagorean tradition considered studying and meditating on Mathematics, Geometry, Astronomy and Astrology to be among the highest of spiritual disciplines, leading to getting a sense of the living shape and power of the mind of the Source.

Meditating on number, or on the meaning of simple geometric shapes like triangles, can be a powerful form of prayer. Contrary to our modern concept of prayer of meditation, which mostly sets the rational mind aside or attempts to quiet it, Platonic and Pythagorean meditation uses the focus of disciplined Reason to climb from the world of multiplicity and division up to the world of Unitive Reason or Intellect.

Numbers are alive. Ideas are alive. The forms are alive. Using our divinely given human reason we climb from the physical creation around us, up through the creative ideas underlying them, in an unbroken chain leading all the way to the Source and Creator.

Conceived in this way, the study of Astrology mirrors the structure of creation.

> ***The heavens declare the glory of God,***
> ***And the firmament sheweth forth his handiwork.***

Eternal Moral Law

We have good reason for saying there are eternal laws and principles, eternal forms or ideas which form the structural basis of our universe. I think we have similar justification for arguing that there is an eternal natural moral law built in to the structure of the universe.

The line of reasoning I am using here is not original to me. There are examples of this argument in the late platonist philosopher Proclus. Closer to our own age the great British writer G K Chesterton uses similar logic, as does C S Lewis. The classic book by Lewis, *The Abolition of Man*, is an extended argument on this topic, and I strongly recommended it. While Lewis is best known as being a Christian apologist, this book is not specifically Christian and argues for a cross-cultural moral law common to most human societies across the world.

Consider this situation.

We are sitting across a table from each other. I reach over, take your wallet, and remove your money and credit card and say, "I'll take these, thank you." If you try to protest I punch you in the mouth and tell you to shut up.

I can predict with a very high level of confidence that you would find my acts there to be immoral, abhorrent, disgusting - and rightly so. You would likely say that is is unfair to steal another person's property and to use violence to do it. In any civilized society you should be able to assume that, and you assume that anyone who acts in such a way should be restrained and punished.

Precisely that is my point.

In order to object to my actions, you appeal to a moral law. You would say that it is just understood that stealing is a moral violation, as is the use of violence without provocation. For that appeal to make sense, there needs to be a standard outside of us, a real moral law that you can point to. This law exists independently of our individual feelings or thoughts or opinions, and we assume that any sane and reasonable human being would assent to that law without the need for explanation or argument.

Such a law is just assumed; it goes without saying. Try to think of not assuming that - try to think of stealing and violence being okay - and it twists your mind in knots. For me, to try to think that way feels like I am going against the very structure of my mind. It feels painful, it feels self-contradictory, it hurts.

We cannot judge anything as moral or immoral without there being an agreed-upon common standard we can point to. Without that common standard we have no grounds for judging other than how we feel - and feelings are not solid ground for moral judgments.

If you try to use feelings to make your case here, you might argue that my stealing and attacking you makes you feel violated and abused. I could easily respond, Big deal, I feel richer and more powerful now. It is my feelings against yours. Even to try to make that case using feelings you would need to appeal to a moral law that says that deliberately causing harm or hurting a person's feelings is wrong and immoral. In such a case it's my feelings against yours; my truth against your truth. Who's to judge?

You can't make moral judgments at all without an agreed upon standard to point to and judge by. We use words like justice, and fairness, and respect, and those words have no meaning at all unless there is a standard to point to that defines them.

In our terms here, Justice and Fairness and Respect are all Platonic forms, eternal ideas that are part of the structural underpinning of the universe. Our human concepts of Justice, Fairness and Respect are attempts to mirror and understand those eternal laws.

Try to imagine a world where you cannot assume that Justice and Fairness and Respect all exist as real standards... and what you end up

Eternal Moral Law

with something very much like the modern scientific concept of an external universe that is completely value-free, where all questions of value are subjective to human beings, values we impose on the world rather than their being inherent in the world. In such a world there is no eternal truth, and everything is relative.

If you really think through the implications of that, such a world is a frightening empty horror.

Consider a world where you can't assume that people just understand that it is wrong to steal, or to use violence on a person. In such a world, you have only one standard to go by - physical force. The strong do what they want, and the weak have to put up with it. I find the thought of such a world to be absolutely abhorrent, sheer horror, and I assume that you do too. I also think you can fairly describe such a world as subhuman. In *The Abolition of Man* C S Lewis has a lengthy section examining agreed upon moral laws as recorded in cultures from all over the world. In that book the name that Lewis gives to this law is the Tao. He demonstrates that there is a remarkable cross-cultural consistency in the case of many ethical laws.

There are differences between cultures in some specific areas of morality. There are some subjects, most notably sexual roles and relations, where you can find very different standards cross culturally. That does not negate the large areas of common consent across culture and history.

To wrap up this argument, consider Saturn's place in the traditional cosmos. Saturn is at the border between the eternal and temporal worlds, and Saturn mirrors the eternal laws down into our world. Many of the meanings of Saturn fall on these lines of judgment, the law, consequences for actions, justice, punishment, duty, responsibility and so on.

Our changing world of space and time is built on eternal structural principles, eternal laws. Saturn mirrors those laws and their consequences into our experience in time.

We do indeed always exist in two worlds, time and eternity, and we are always judged by eternal moral and physical laws in all our thoughts and actions, and at every moment of our lives. The temporal mirrors the eternal - and though our mirrors are not perfect, that is not a good reason for smashing all mirrors and arguing that they are useless and mere subjective opinion.

The Living Law

Normally, when we think of laws or statutes or commandments, this brings to mind something dry, legalistic, dusty and mechanical, like the clauses of a legal document. In terms of what we are talking about here those connotations are all reflections of our modern usage, and they are distortions. This does not begin to approach what the Living Law is all about.

To give something of the flavor of what I am talking about, look in the Bible at those passages in the psalms that speak of the Law. The psalms use metaphors describing the law as being alive, being sweet, feeding and satisfying the soul, and so on. You will also see the metaphor of Wisdom as a Person, and of the Law as a living being. In far eastern thought this has a parallel in the concept of the Tao, the Way, a living and flexible structure.

This sense of the Law as a living being includes within it qualities of caring and mercy and compassion. We tend to think of law as over against mercy, but the two concepts belong together, they are intertwined to the point of being indistinguishable.

Here I want to share my own personal experience. I want to talk about what it is like to meet the Living Law in my prayers and meditations.

There are many passages in Platonic writing describing the One and the Good as the source of all, and of the divine Intellect mirroring eternal law and order in our minds and in the universe around us. Reading those passages I feel I am coming to meet a living glowing being of unimaginable order, beauty and intensity. The words connect me to something alive.

I have also meditated on the biblical Psalms talking about the Law, and I understand what they mean when it is called beautiful, nourishing, sweet, desirable and attractive above all else. I have experienced all of those in within me during my prayers. I understand when the psalms say that those who have found the law are like trees with deep roots, and those who ignore the law are like insubstantial chaff which the wind blows away. A life without the living law lacks all substance, depth, and reality. Physically it is like trying to nourish your body on potato chips, candy bars and Coke. There is a depth of nourishment and sustenance to the Law that reaches down into the heart of my being. I now need my time with the Living Law as much or more than I need my breakfast and tea in the morning. Without it I feel I am being spiritually starved and left rootless.

When I talk about the eternal laws and structures of mathematics and geometry that govern the movements of the planets, I want to convey a sense of the awe, beauty and wonder of interacting with something alive and dancing, of living in the body of dynamic and caring being. I now feel a similar sense of awe and wonder, of living intelligence, of caring and of gratitude, when I really think deeply about Justice being a living structural principle that is hard-wired into the essence of the universe. I now understand that Justice is alive in the fullest sense of the term.

As another way to approach this, take some time to read the first half dozen or so chapters of the Book of Proverbs. Get a feel for the kind of person they are describing, and the kind of life they say is worthwhile. Try to imagine what a society would be like if most of its people were committed to living by those laws. Then pause a bit, and try to imagine what a society would be like if those qualities were completely missing, or if those values were belittled or ignored. I think that exercise will give something of a feel for what I am trying to get at when I talk of a living law wired into the universe itself.

With the Living Law the universe is a thing of order and beauty. of worth and of value. Without that law we inhabit an empty chaos, a world of meaningless and hostile shells, a hell.

One is a living world, the other a dead world.

Saturn and the Golden Age

The quote we will examine in this essay is from book 4 of Plato's *Laws*. The translation here is by Thomas Taylor, who substitutes the Roman god name Saturn for the original Greek Zeus. I have changed some of the wording based on more modern translations where Taylor's translation might be unclear or misleading because of the changes in meaning of words since his time. The speaker here is describing a previous golden age which was under the rulership of Saturn. The emphases in the text are mine.

> GUEST. A long time then prior to those habitations of cities which we have before discussed, a certain government and habitation is said to have subsisted under Saturn; a government extremely happy, and of which the present aristocracies are an imitation.
>
> We learn, then, from the report of the blessed life of the inhabitants of that time, that they possessed all things in abundance, and spontaneously produced; of which the following is said to be the cause: **Saturn**, well knowing (as we have already observed) that no human nature, when endued with absolute dominion, is so sufficient to itself as not to be filled with insolence and injustice, in consequence of understanding this, **placed over our cities, as kings and governors, not men, but daemons of a more divine and excellent kind**; just as we do at present with flocks of sheep and herds of tame cattle. For we do not make oxen governors of oxen, nor goats of goats; but we ourselves rule over them, as being of a better race.
>
> In a similar manner this God, who is a lover of mankind, placed over us the race of daemons, as being more excellent than our species. But these taking care of our concerns, with great facility both to themselves and us, imparted to us peace, respect for others, liberty and abundance of justice,

and a state of happiness and harmony among the races of the world.

This our present discourse, therefore, employing truth, asserts, that such cities as are not governed by a divinity, but by some mortal, will never be exempt from evils and labours: but it is our opinion that we ought, by all possible means, to imitate the life which is said to have been under Saturn; and that, being obedient to as much of immortality as is inherent in our nature, we should govern both publicly and privately our houses and cities, calling law the distribution of intellect.

For, if one man, or a certain oligarchy, or democracy, possessing a soul aspiring after pleasures and desires, and requiring to be filled with these, but not being able to retain them, should be tormented with insatiable vicious desires; such a one, when governing either a city or an individual, would trample on the laws; and, as we just now said, under such a dominion there could be no possibility of obtaining safety.

Humanity cannot live as a law to itself; our proper place is within the overall Great Chain of Being, where we look to the levels above us, and ultimately to the Source of All, for our guidance, our direction, our sense of judgment. In the overall order, we in turn have an obligation to direct and care for the levels in the chain below us, to treat animals, and all living beings including the earth, with care and respect.

In the Platonic cosmos the level of the Daemons served as a bridge, a mediator between our human souls and the higher gods. The Christian concept of Guardian Angel is pointing at a similar level of reality. We get in trouble when we cease looking to higher levels in the chain, and let ourselves be led by our own desire and ambition. When we do that, we cease to treat each other well, and are under the dominion of our appetites.

Saturn and the Golden Age

This makes some important points. First of there is the need for respect for a higher law, a sense of submitting to a law above us and having a respectful care for the levels below us. This means that we as rational creatures are able to think and to judge, and we are responsible for governing and directing our own desires within the larger context of order.

This includes a respect for the teachings and traditions passed down by those who have gone before us. There are similar levels of respect and obedience within the family structure, where children should be led by their parents. Parents are obligated to show reverence for their elders, the grand-parents, and to care for their children's best interests and guide them in learning the guidance of the higher laws. In a well ordered political state citizens owe obedience to their rulers, and the rulers in turn are obligated to act for the greatest well being of the citizens.

This makes a very important point: **When this system is working, each level owes respect and obedience to the level above it, and owes care, guidance and nurturing to the level below it.**

When these rules are not followed, it breaks the whole chain of order and throws the entire structure - of society, of the family, of our individual lives - into a disorderly, exploitive and vicious chaos. A selfish and corrupt government destroys respect for government and for laws. Selfish and uncaring parents destroy respect for the family and breed rebellion in children, who follow their own whims since they feel they cannot trust the intentions of their elders.

Humanity is not wise or mature enough to be a law unto itself. Humanity needs a higher law, higher guidance, in order to flourish. Without that higher guidance humanity destroys itself by its own lower nature.

There is another important reason that this chain of being is needed: the higher levels also nurture and feed the levels below - recall our previous discussion on the Living Law. It is a kind of nourishment that we need to flourish. Break the chain and something inside of us is starved. Deprived of our proper higher spiritual nourishment, we turn to lower level substitutes to try to fill that need, and it doesn't work, it creates an insatiable vicious circle that self-destructs.

The system of laws and guidance that is being passed down is not a dry and dead set of regulations and ordinances, it is a living, breathing and divine entity that has a life of its own and that guides us, feeds us, nourishes and cares for us. Without that living connection we are rootless, we wither, dry up and blow away.

In traditional astrology part of the purpose of Saturn is to remind us of our place in the chain, the responsibilities we have, and the laws we must follow to be in harmony with each other and with the larger universe.

Cycles of Time and Eternity

In our survey of the assumptions of our modern world view we saw that there is an implicit inner-outer disconnect and opposition. The isolated individual, with their inner world of private psychological meaning, is pitted over against a value-free or even hostile external world. This gives us a basic stance of inner versus outer, individual versus collective.

This inner-outer opposition is a significant component of much of modern astrology, and I want to examine a particularly clearly stated example here. The following quotes are from The *Practice of Astrology* by Dane Rudhyar. Rudhyar is a proponent of a new, humanistic, person centered astrology that he defines as over against what he conceives as the old fatalistic model. And the new, of course, is superior and more evolved. I think that, like many modern astrologers, he is unfairly caricaturing and attacking traditional astrology without really understanding it; we already addressed that issue with some of the modern astrologers we looked at.

Rudhyar views the purpose of astrology, and of human life, as the unfolding of human potential. His work has had an enormous influence on mainstream modern astrology including some of the people we looked at, including Liz Greene, Isabel Hickey and Steven Forrest.

I am using this passage from Rudhyar because I think it clearly lays out the inner-outer opposition. I also think Rudhyar misunderstands the full nature of cycles, and we will address that after we look at this passage.

As you read these quotes, take into account that Rudhyar came of age around the time of World War One and the birth of communist Russia, and began his most influential work during the 1930's, the era of the rise of Nazi Germany and other totalitarian states, leading up to World War Two and its aftermath. That background helps to explain his stance.

Cycles of Time and Eternity

The following quotes are from the chapter in *The Practice of Astrology* on transits. The bold emphasis is by me, italic emphasis is from Rudhyar's original text.

> **The birth-chart does not change**, but the world goes on and celestial bodies pursue their cyclic motions as if nothing had happened. Yet something tremendous happened; **a man has been born with the *potential* ability to stop time** in himself and to immortalize the structure of his selfhood - the structure patterned after the entire sky at the moment of his first breath. If he succeeds in so doing, he becomes, actually and as a living human personality, his own sky - that is, God's projection upon earth of one phase of His universal being at one moment of time. **Individual immortality is thus the overcoming of the constant fatality of change by something which resists change** - or, abstractly speaking, the overcoming of time by space. **This means also the overcoming of 'Nature' by 'self'**, for self is the unchanging identity of the individual - the 'I', and the 'I" is fundamentally the stable structure of being to which every changing factor has to be referred if there is to be *consciousness*.
>
> ...Astrologically speaking, this means that the integrity of our birth-chart should be maintained against the pressure of the universe of change (Nature) - thus, against the further dynamic impact of all the celestial bodies altering their positions after our birth. These constant impacts refer to what astrologers call 'transits'. *A transit is the focused manifestation of the unending pressure applied by Nature upon the natal, archetypal structure of our selfhood.* **It pits the power of the universe of change - and of the collective, social factors in individual experience which constitute 'human nature' - against the integrity of the individual; thus it pits the ephemeris against the birth-chart!**

All transits (except the passages of planets over the places they occupied in the birth-chart) tend to distort and disfigure the basic pattern of our self, to throw it out of balance. They are therefore challenges. If we meet them and remain true to our own archetypal 'truth' (which can be read in the birth-chart), then we have gained greatly in consciousness and power. We have learned, by overcoming change or opposition, more about what we are as a changeless self. We are thus able to live a fuller life, to incarnate more of our self into earth-life, to express more convincingly our character, *to become in act what we are in potentiality* - which is the foundation for 'personal immortality'.

We have several parallel dualisms and oppositions set up in this passage by Rudhyar, and they are characteristic of much of our modern world in general and of modern astrology in particular.

- inner against outer

- individual against collective

- static birth chart against time

- the inner Self against hostile Nature

- the lone individual against restricting society

Also note that Rudhyar explicitly states that individual identity is unchanging, that it is frozen in time in the birth chart.

In popular modern astrology, this opposition of individual against collective is symbolized by the opposition of Uranus against Saturn - new against old, individual against collective, human potential against restricting outer forms, the lone freedom fighter against the repressive collective state.

The rebel, the heretic, the protester - the Protestant.

Cycles of Time and Eternity

To examine this point further I want to look at quotes from a student of Rudhyar's, Alexander Ruperti. These are from the book *Cycles of Becoming: The Humanistic Approach*. I am including these because they make explicit a political dimension to this inner-outer split. In Ruperti's system progressions indicate an unfolding of potential from within, while transits are the hostile effect of the outer world upon the person. Inner versus outer.

Emphases in bold are by me.

> Everything that surrounds the individual in life (described by the transit cycle) will tend to change the quality of his essential being. Day by day his integrity will be challenged. **All of those factors which the transits refer to will draw him away from the essence of his true identity...**
>
> **The degree and quality of *resistance* an individual will have to the pressures and forces of the environment** is difficult to ascertain. In addition to the socio-cultural traditions, racial or nationalistic loyalties and the subtle or harsh commands of public opinion as expressed through the mass-media (especially in its advertisements), a person is also bombarded by solar and cosmic radiation...
>
> **Man must be attacked from without (transits)** at a time when he is weak within (progressions) and otherwise unsupported, if his resistance against the constant pressure of society and the universe is to collapse.
>
> Collective values and collective fate weigh heavily on each individual in a so-called 'modern' society, and especially on those living in large cities...

Here the inner-outer war is very explicitly laid out. We have the solitary individual fighting the external forces of nature, of cosmic radiation, of the mass media, of popular tradition, and of the weight of public opinion - the lone individual ranged over against the entire collective universe! I think that Ruperti's use of the word *resistance* carries connotations of its use during the Nazi era, as referring to people in Europe attempting to fight totalitarian oppression. This is the stance of the lone individual fighting for identity against a hostile system and a hostile universe.

Ruperti and Rudhyar both did some marvelous work, and Ruperti's work on cycles as showing unfolding of human potential is very valuable, but I think their work is marred by this inner-outer disconnect and hostility. I also think it is a misunderstanding of cycles and of transits. They are both so very, very close to seeing the whole picture.

I want to present a different way of viewing transits. I first saw this concept in a book called *How to Rectify a birth chart* by Laurie Efrein, and the concept is summed up in the title of the initial chapter, *How a Lifetime of Astrology is Built-In at Birth*.

Recall that we talked about how you can draw up a birth chart for any given date, time and location thousands of years into the past and future. Given that same logic, at the time of birth, you can draw up the transits for the entire lifetime. They are already there, given what we know of the planetary positions and the laws of planetary movement.

Consider that: at birth, you have the entire unfolding set of transits, progressions, solar returns and any other predictive technique you care to use, already there, implicit in the birth chart and the structure of cycles through time. The whole framework of life experience is already potentially mapped out at the moment of birth.

I think it makes far more sense to say that the transits are every bit as much a part of the potential of the birth chart as are progressions. There is no place at which you can draw the line between inner and outer. They are together all part of a seamless whole. The same logical system of mathematics produces both progressions and transits - and remember, both progressions and transits use the same ephemeris!

The human life is not just a static birth chart. The human life is the entire process of birth chart, plus progressions, plus transits, plus actual life experience, all unfolding through time. The full identity is shown by the *entire* cycle, not just the moment of birth. Full human identity is part of the larger whole, not over against it.

This is the critical error that Rudhyar made. Human identity is **not** frozen at the moment in time of the birth chart. It makes more sense to view the birth chart as a seed point or pattern that is a starting framework for further development rather than a static unchanging identity to be defended against change. The purpose of human life is not to stop time, but to work with and in time.

A child is not born into the world to fight the world. A child comes into this world in order to be part of the world, to change and grow, to go through the entire cycle from birth to death, and perhaps beyond.

Children are born into the world as part of the world, not over against the world.

Human identity is never static and frozen. We grow, we change, we have experiences and respond to them, we make choices and deal with the consequences. The birth chart, plus progressions, plus transits, plus circumstances, together all form the dynamic framework within which human life is played out. It is a framework that includes an element of free will within an overall organic structure.

The core principle of the Platonic system, that the eternal order and identity is revealed in the entire temporal cycle, applies equally to human life, and here the eternal order is shown in the structure through time of all of the charts and predictive techniques, including transits, including progressions, including primary directions or profections or any other predictive technique you care to use. We need to see the entire cycle play out in time in order to grasp what is implicit all at once in the eternal order outside of time.

Rudhyar and Ruperti come so very close to this truth in their concepts of cycles and unfolding. Instead of it being individual over against

Cycles of Time and Eternity

collective, inner over against outer, it is far more true to say that both are part of larger system including both, and that the larger system mirrors the eternal structural principles of the universe. Eternity is mirrored in the unfolding of time. Saturn's structure has to include time as well as space to be able to mirror entire cycles, and many of the meanings of Saturn have to do with the passage of time.

Eternity is mirrored in entire cycles in time, and the planet Saturn represents that boundary between eternity and time. Many of Saturn's meanings grow out of this central concept.

Saturn and Ouranos

This is a good place to address the enormous impact in modern astrology of having the outer planet Uranus be in an orbit beyond that of Saturn.

For most of this section I will spell the name of the Greek god as Ouranos rather than Uranus. I want to avoid immediate association with the modern planet of that name. The word in the original Greek means the Heavens or the Sky. Ouranos and Gaia, or Heaven and Earth, together gave birth to a large number of gods, including Kronus, better known by his Roman name of Saturn.

Ouranos/Uranus in Mythology

In the original Greek mythology Ouranos is the father of Kronus/Saturn. Saturn overthrew the rule of his father by castrating him, and Saturn and his wife Rhea gave birth to other gods, including Zeus, also known as Jupiter. Zeus in turn overthrew and castrated Kronus as Kronus had overthrown and castrated Ouranos.

Ouranos/Uranus in Traditional Astrology

If you consider the symbolism of the traditional cosmos, Ouranos, or the Heavens, is the sphere of the fixed stars that surround the planets. Kronus, the son of Ouranos, is the outermost of the planets, the planet closest to Ouranos. The son of Kronus, Zeus or Jupiter, is the next planet in order. Saturn here in the original mythology has his distinctive place at the border between the realm of the fixed stars and the realm of the perpetually moving planets. Saturn is at the border between time and eternity, and that is reflected in the mythology.

The planet Zeus or Jupiter is a lower level image or representative of the Demiurge, the artisan god who crafted the manifest cosmos we inhabit, looking to the planet Saturn for the patterns or templates on which the cosmos is built. Saturn in this symbolism mirrors the forms and patterns of the eternal world down into the world of time and matter.

Uranus in Modern Astrology

In modern astrology the symbolism of Saturn and Uranus has been flipped on its head. The modern planet Uranus, the next planet out from Saturn in the modern cosmos, is cast in the role of the brave freedom fighter and rebel who fights and overthrows Saturn, and Saturn represents everything old, oppressive, outmoded and restricting.

The original mythology has been reversed. Instead of Saturn overthrowing his father Uranus, we have Uranus the freedom fighter overthrowing Saturn. In terms of the traditional mythology it makes no sense.

Switch of Meanings of Saturn

You can see how this change in mythology has profound effects on the meanings of Saturn, and on the system as a whole. In the traditional system Saturn mirrors the eternal law and structure of The Heavens or Ouranos down into our mutable world. Saturn is associated with eternal law and with tradition, with rules that have been passed down over time. There is a respect and reverence for the traditional laws and structures.

With Uranus in modern astrology Saturn now represents all that is outmoded, outdated, restrictive and no longer useful. Uranus the eternal rebel overthrows Saturn and stands for the new, the young, the modern. Tradition is devalued, as is anything old, as are old people, and everything new and youthful is worshiped and highly valued.

In modern astrology the entire system of tradition on which astrology is originally based is devalued and thrown away, to be replaced by the new and modern. We saw that as a common

Saturn and Ouranos

thread running through the writings from modern astrologers that we examined in the first part of this book.

The discovery of the outer planets did not simply add a couple of new moving bodies orbiting around the Sun. It completely changed the symbolic meaning of the structure of the cosmos. In this book I am arguing that much of value has been thrown away with this switch of meaning, and I also argue for reclaiming much of the traditional meaning, of the order of the Cosmos in general, and of the meaning of Saturn in particular.

Consistency in Astrology

I want to add another dimension to our argument that there is an eternal order, an eternal set of structural principles to the universe, and that our minds can apprehend and mirror that order. That dimension is the fact of the very amazing consistency of meaning in many of the aspects of astrology over the ages.

For all that I am emphasizing the changes in meaning of Saturn and the other planets in the last century, there is still an astounding consistency of meaning to the symbolism. Saturn is still recognizably Saturn. You could never mistake Saturn for Venus. If we look at the earliest meanings for Saturn, from Valens, Firmicus Maternus and other classic authors, these rules and attributions still apply, they still work, sometimes frighteningly well. If you look at the modern meanings attributed to Saturn they still all have a close family resemblance to the earliest set of meanings. They point to the same underlying core reality.

I maintain that this is a very strong argument for saying that the system of astrology mirrors something in the actual structure of the universe. It is not simply a human created construct. This is also a very strong argument for remembering that we still have much to learn from traditional concepts like benefic and malefic, and dignity and debility, even if such concepts are unpopular in our modern culture and we would prefer to think that everything in our astrology must by definition be interpreted positively. In fact I think it is precisely because modern astrology has such a positive slant that we have much to learn from the traditional concepts. They provide a balance and an alternate perspective.

Astrology changes and develops over time, but this does not invalidate the tradition. Rather, it builds on it. We are passing down a sacred tradition, and I am arguing for maintaining the fullness of the tradition - and that is a very Saturnian sort of thing to do.

The Sphere of Saturn and Astrology

Another window into the meaning of Saturn in the traditional world is shown in the following quote from Dante Alighieri, the Italian writer best known as author of the *Divine Comedy*. In the *Convivio* Dante compares the seven liberal arts to the seven planets, assigning them as follows.

- Grammar corresponds to the Moon,
- Logic to Mercury,
- Rhetoric to Venus,
- Arithmetic to the Sun,
- Music to Mars,
- Geometry to Jupiter,
- ***and Astrology to Saturn.***

Here is the quote from Dante.

> The heaven of Saturn has two properties by which it may be compared to Astrology: one is the slowness of its movement through the 12 signs, for according to the writings of the astrologers, a time of more than 29 years is required for its revolution; the other is that it is high above all the other planets. And these two properties are found in Astrology: for in completing its circle (that is to say, to master this science) a very great span of time passes, both because of its handmaids, which are more numerous than those of any of the above-mentioned sciences, and because of the experience required in it for making proper judgments. Furthermore, it is far higher than all the others, since, as Aristotle says at the beginning of On the Soul, a science is high in nobility by virtue of the nobility of its subject and by

The Sphere of Saturn and Astrology

virtue of its certainty; and this one, more than any of those mentioned above, is high and noble because of its high and noble subject, which regards the movement of the heaven, and high and noble because of its certainty, which is flawless, as coming from a most perfect and regular principle. And if anyone believes that there is a flaw in it, it does not pertain to the science, but as Ptolemy says, it results from our negligence, and so must be attributed to that.

In this quote the art and science of Astrology is attributed to the planet Saturn. This fits well in the context of Saturn's overall meaning that we have been developing. Astrology is a crowning and integrating science showing how the world of eternal order plays out in our temporal world. It fits in with the core meanings of Saturn given its position on the border of time and eternity, and Saturn's association with the cycles of time.

Living in Two Worlds

In order to complete our Platonic model of the cosmos, we need to talk about the nature of the human being, and how we fit in this world.

The cosmos has an eternal dimension and a temporal dimension. There is a common law to both, a common set of structural principles that Plato called the Forms or Ideas. These structural Forms also include basic moral standards hard-wired into the universe, standards that we describe with words like Justice.

As living and rational creatures we as human beings live in both worlds at the same time. There is our identity here in time, and there is the part of us that always lives in eternity that is sometimes described as our Soul. This model of the human is a common feature of the traditional cosmos, and we also see it reflected in most if not all of the modern astrologers we have looked. When you speak of life after death, or of reincarnation and multiple lives, this implies that there is a part of us which is outside of the world of life and death and that continues to exist between lives.

What is distinctive about the Platonic model is that the part of us as human beings that provides the bridge between the eternal and temporal worlds is our ability to Reason.

I put Reason with a capital letter here to point to a primary human faculty, that which makes us distinctly human and distinguishes us from other animals. Reason is related to the word Ratio which means to measure and balance. Our reason is what gives us the ability to measure, evaluate, choose and judge, and to do that correctly Reason needs a standard, a measuring stick to judge by. That standard is rooted in the eternal world, so Reason correctly used integrates both worlds and brings the eternal standards into our life in time.

I think this emphasis on reason is very different from many modern connotations of the word soul. Soul is much more likely to be thought of as a matter of feeling - we are immortal because we somehow feel

Living in Two Worlds

that is true. Similarly, in order to connect with the divine it is characteristic of modern spirituality to conceive that as involving setting aside the busy rational mind and tuning in to our wordless feelings to make the connection.

In the Platonic model of the world, the eternal dimension is not warm, fuzzy and formless. It has an eternal structure. The part of our minds that connects to this eternal structure is what we call Intellect or Unitive Knowing, All-At-Once knowing. Our Reason connects to the Intellect, and the job of reason is to shape our minds, our judgments, along the lines of the eternal Forms.

In this model the most important purpose of human life is to judge, and to act in alignment with the Eternal Law that is hard wired in the cosmos and in the structure of our minds. That is the theme of many of the Platonic dialogues, and is the central subject of *The Republic*. This is why it is so very important for us to have a strong, living sense of the cosmos having built-in eternal laws. Without that, all our astrology, and all of our lives, are just a matter of shapeless feelings, shifting images in clouds and smoke that come and go.

In the model of traditional astrology Saturn is the bridge between the two worlds. Saturn mirrors the eternal structures down into the changing world of space and time. That is why we associate Saturn with concepts like Law, and Justice, and Judgment. Saturn often relates to dealing with the consequences of our choices and actions. The eternal laws we point to with Saturn aren't warm, fuzzy and formless, they are hard, structured and definite.

All of our acts have consequences because we are judged by these eternal laws every moment of our lives. We are judged during our lives, and we are judged after death. Every model of life after death or reincarnation that I have ever seen includes the idea that our fate after death is a consequence of the choices we make in this life. Our next life is determined by the present life.

Saturn at the border of time and eternity reminds us that the eternal law is always there, and that we face that law at death. Using a common traditional metaphor, at death we face judgment. I believe that this judgment includes mercy, and that the concepts of Love and Mercy also point to eternal forms. We need Mercy and Judgment together.

We now have all the elements of the traditional cosmos in place, so we have a context within which the full meaning of Saturn can make sense in our modern world. Given this structure, we are ready to look at some of the different important dimensions of the meaning of Saturn. I want to concentrate on concepts that are either under-emphasized or not usually dealt with in modern astrology. I am going for balance, which is a very Saturnian thing to do.

Part Three - Essays on Saturn Themes

Introduction

This section is not about how to interpret Saturn in a chart; it is about the kinds of themes that come up when you are dealing with Saturn related events. We are at the level of ideas and philosophy rather than interpretation.

The experiences associated with Saturn are complex. More than any other planet it plumbs the depths of evil, and the depths of good. We need to deal with both. Our modern world has a tendency to want to deny or hide the unpleasant truths of experience that Saturn can bring into our lives. Part of Saturn's meaning has to do with shadows, blind spots, things hidden, shunned and feared. We will bring some of those experiences out of the shadows and look at how our lives are richer because of them.

Balance

The concept of balance has been largely lost in our culture of continuous growth, expansion and improvement. We no longer think in terms of balanced concepts but of single unbalanced concepts we seek to push to an extreme. Here the full traditional meaning of Saturn is particularly useful, as it is, by definition, the opposition, the reaction, the balance to things that are out of control in an extreme direction.

Key Concepts

There are a few key concepts that explain the core of meanings attributed to Saturn, and these are also core structural concepts for all of the astrology system.

There is the concept of oppositions and balance. Some of the core meanings of Saturn are related to its being in opposition, or over against, or blocking, or balancing.

There are the paired concepts of time and eternity, with time mirroring the structure of eternity, and Saturn being at the pivot point between the two. Some of the meanings of Saturn point to eternal things like law and judgment, and some point to the effects of time, and some meanings combine the two, so that you have judgment or reckoning in time.

Take these concepts together and you have cycles of alternating opposites in motion over time. Time mirrors eternity only in the entire cycle. This connects to other Saturnian qualities: the wisdom of age, learning from experience, learning from history, the vantage point of the entire cycle balancing the blind spots of the current fads, and so on. Few points in cycle of time are completely balanced, but the cycle as a whole expresses balance. There is a pendulum in motion, swinging back and forth. Part of the purpose of this section is to bring this lack of balance to awareness, and then to focus on some specific subject areas that are weak and unbalanced in our culture.

A Culture of One-Sided Extremes

We have a culture that consistently values one-sided extremes and judges in terms of More and Less. In terms of opposites, we consistently see our culture wanting to embrace and focus on one side of a pair, and ignore or denigrate or deny or otherwise not see the other side. We value one side and not the other. We live in a culture of More is Better, a quantity culture. We know how to deal with more, we don't deal well with less.

The modern astrologers we looked at share the view that the purpose of life is to do fulfill our potential. We are here to be as happy and wealthy and strong and successful and long lived as we possibly can, all phrased in terms of superlatives.

These examples show how this lack of balance runs like a golden thread all through our culture.

- We value youth and not age.

- We are comfortable with birth and not comfortable with death, which we tend to gloss over or deny. We know how to be born and grow well, and we have lost the art of aging and dying well.

- We are good at expanding and not at contracting. We are good at growing and not good at dealing with decaying.

- We know how to deal with being on the way up and do not know how to navigate being on the way down. We can cope with success and don't deal well with failure.

- We are good at dealing with health and not with handling disease. We can handle comfort and not suffering; we don't know the graceful art of how to suffer well.

- We know how to be proud, and we have forgotten how to be humble.

- We value freedom and we have forgotten the value of constraint.

- We all want to be rich and affluent, and we have forgotten the value of being poor and of humble means.

- We value being famous, and we have lost the power of being anonymous.

- We know how to win and don't know how to lose. We expect things to go our way, and we don't know how to deal with it gracefully when things don't go our way.

- We know how to start things and not how to end them.

The Waning Side of the Cycle

Thinking in terms of cycles, we have lost a sense of the meaning and usefulness of the waning side of cycles. The waxing side is where grow and act, the waning side is where we pull back, reflect and learn. The waxing side is about doing, the waning side is about understanding.

We value learning in order to act, and we have forgotten the worth of learning for its own sake, that action is not completed until it is transmuted into learning. We read without reflecting, which is like eating without digesting. Our entire emphasis is on doing /building /expanding, and we have lost the art of processing /learning /harvesting /distilling.

We know how to be active and not how stop to reflect. There is a very important rhythm to life of alternating action and reflection. We know how to act but not how to stop acting and reflect.

We will pick up this topic of unbalance again in the chapter on time.

We have also forgotten what I think of as the paradox of opposites, highlighted in some religious traditions, where the one who would be Master of all must be Servant of all, where the Highest takes the form of the Lowest. We have forgotten the power of Mary in the Christian tradition where she answers the angel Gabriel by saying, behold the slave of the Lord, be it done unto me according to thy word. We have forgotten that it is equally valuable and worthy to be a good servant as a good master - and, that a good master or leader should be the servant of those under them.

Most important of all is our cultural need to recover the value of the sweet spot, the balance, the middle position, as being the best, the most desirable and the most powerful. We have forgotten that we need the concept of balance to have a powerful concept of quality and of virtue.

Eternal Values

This discussion ties back to the entire second section of this book where we discussed eternal law, including eternal moral law.

We have forgotten how to ask questions of meaning because we don't have a standard to measure meaning against.

Here I want to look back to Aristotle and the Nicomachean Ethics, and the concept of the golden mean. In Aristotle's thinking all of the virtues are a matter of correct balance, and each virtue has a pair of corresponding vices which are unbalanced in opposite directions. We have lost that whole notion of balance, of virtue, of what the Good is. The concepts of virtue, of moral law, and of balance all complement and complete each other.

Given our culture of More is Better, a culture of quantity, we have completely lost the notion that the good of life is Character and Virtue, which is aligning with eternal law. Thinking in terms of our discussion of time and eternity, character focuses on what we bring forward after death into eternal life. In Platonic thought, and in Christian and many other traditions, the only things we are ever judged by is our virtues - not our bank account, not our string of successes, not our healthy body, not how long we lived, not how rich we were, not how famous we were.

Many of the balance problems I listed earlier in this essay trace back to our culture lacking the Saturnian virtues. This includes patience and humility. This also includes the perspective that comes with age, time and experience, the ability to stop and think slowly and deeply. Much of our culture lacks depth, another distinctly Saturnian quality.

Saturn and Time

Many of the meanings of Saturn have to do with time, and the effects of time. Some of the negative effects associated with Saturn - things getting old, or decaying, or falling apart, or declining - are all directly the effects of time. In terms of cycles the distinctly Saturn effects come in late in the cycle. Saturn is associated with decline rather than growth, age rather than youth, decaying rather than growing. falling rather than rising.

Testing

Part of the effect of time is to test things, to try things, to see how well they are built or put together. It also tests the effects of age. Even well built structures eventually fall apart.

Saturn also has to do with consequences. The first Saturn return is often about becoming aware of the things we have built and the choices we have made, and how we deal with the consequences of those choices through time.

Choices and actions are related to structures. If a person chooses a particular career, or a particular marriage, that is a structure. It gives shape to our lives in a good sense, and it also confines us. Once it starts to have effects we are confined to dealing with the consequences of those effects.

Choices also relate to momentum, which is also Saturnian. Once you get into a career and a job, you build up momentum - a skill set, a salary, a reputation - and it is difficult to change career areas once you are established in one area. Trying to change careers can feel like

Balance

stepping off of a moving train; all of the momentum of your career life is moving in that one direction, and switching to a new career isn't just starting over, it is moving against all that momentum. Your job history is part of your resume, and it will follow you for the rest of your life.

It is the same with habits, both good and bad. If you get used to repeatedly grabbing the chocolate ice cream out of the freezer for one last dish before you go to bed, it is more and more likely that the ice cream will jump out of the freezer at you tomorrow. The more often you choose in a single direction, the easier and more likely it is that your next choice will be in that same direction. Building a new habit also includes a struggle against the momentum of the old habit.

This is related to the one-way movement of time, and to the permanence of history. Once you have done something you have done it, and you cannot undo it. We are made aware of this effect in an intensified way with the ubiquity of the internet and of social media. Once you put something out on the web - a post, a picture, a video - it is out there forever for anyone to discover. It is unfortunate that digging up old dirt is often used as a political tactic to destroy reputations, so that a thoughtless or immature comment you made in high school can come back 40 years later to be held against you. History can be relentless, and Time is relentless - and people, especially in faceless crowds, can be very harsh and relentless in how they use time. Judging in this harsh way is a good example of Saturn as malefic.

> *The Moving Finger writes; and, having writ,*
> *Moves on: nor all thy Piety nor Wit*
> *Shall lure it back to cancel half a Line,*
> *Nor all thy Tears wash out a Word of it.*
> - Omar Khayyam, translated by Edgar Fitzgerald

Good Effects of Structure

In the previous section I talked mainly about structure and habits as being confining, but the opposite is true also. Building structure and momentum through time is also a way to accomplish worthwhile things.

Building a career takes time, it takes learning, it takes experience, it takes work and character. All of those together create a worthwhile structure that has its own positive momentum.

Raising a child well takes time. That process is aided by a stable family structure to support it, a strong stable relationship. Raising a child well takes forethought, planning and careful decision, and deliberate repeated action, and all of those are Saturnian sorts of skills.

Mastering a system like astrology takes time. If you are serious about astrology you should count on at least a good ten years of study, research and practice to assimilate the system to the point that you can do it well. The process of learning focuses on myriad details over time, until you reach the point of having all-at-once knowledge of the system, a unitive understanding. That synthesis gives the perspective to know what meanings to apply to a given situation.

The process of learning and mastering anything worthwhile takes a great deal of time, of work and sustained discipline, and it develops a depth of understanding that comes with mastery. It also takes a lot of patience and of perseverance. All of those are particularly Saturnian qualities.

History

Another positive side to the movement of time through history is historical awareness, learning from time and experience. Our modern culture has largely lost a sense of history, the value of knowing it, of respecting it, and of learning from it.

Related to this is the value of paying attention to what has been passed down through history, of reverence for tradition as a cumulative human experience. Tradition passes on what has stood the test of time.

This relates to the connection of Saturn with moving in cycles. Historical awareness teaches us we don't understand the meaning of the whole until we see the entire cycle. We don't understand an action until we see it play out in time. This in turn is related to time as mirroring eternal order, learning that the results of our actions follow laws. We can only see that when we can see the whole order, and that takes time. Saturn is the structure of space and time together. An awareness of history increases awareness of the whole structure.

The Wisdom of Time and Age

This is a very rich concept, and it ties in a lot of the dimensions of Saturn's meaning.

Part of the wisdom of age comes with having lived long enough that you have seen fads and fashions come and go, and then return again. You've lived long enough to have watched rises and falls in power and reputation. You learn that history is not a straight line of progress; it involves cycles of up and down, back and forth. Political parties ride waves of popularity and are voted into power, only to be voted out of power down the road when their wave ebbs, and the opposite party's wave is rising and cresting. There is a rhythm back and forth, a dance and play of opposites. That is the wisdom that comes with awareness of whole cycles in time.

Cycles and "Progress"

The following quote is from Ecclesiastes. This passage made its way into pop music history when The Byrds made it a hit single with their song *Turn, Turn, Turn*. As you read it over, consider how much of this goes against the grain of our culture, and how this passage on cycles resonates with the earlier section on balance.

Balance

Ecclesiastes, Chapter 3, King James Version

1 To every thing there is a season, and a time to every purpose under the heaven:
2 A time to be born, and a time to die; a time to plant, and a time to pluck up that which is planted;
3 A time to kill, and a time to heal; a time to break down, and a time to build up;
4 A time to weep, and a time to laugh; a time to mourn, and a time to dance;
5 A time to cast away stones, and a time to gather stones together; a time to embrace, and a time to refrain from embracing;
6 A time to get, and a time to lose; a time to keep, and a time to cast away;
7 A time to rend, and a time to sew; a time to keep silence, and a time to speak;
8 A time to love, and a time to hate; a time of war, and a time of peace.

Notice how this passage moves back and forth, in pairs of opposites. This is the antithesis of our culture's ideal of perpetual progress. Cyclic pairs describe how human history actually works out across time - not what *should* happen, or what we would *like* to happen, but what actually *does* happen.

A lot of our culture is built on the assumption of perpetual straight line growth and progress, unending improvement going on into the future. Saturn teaches us that reality doesn't work out like that. Reality isn't shaped like a straight line; it is wavy, going up and down, back and forth, around and around through time.

There is a wisdom and maturity that comes with recognizing that. There is wisdom in being able to recognize what phase of a cycle you are in - waxing or waning, growing or pulling back - and adjusting your attitude and your actions accordingly. It is easy to deal with the political party you support winning an election, and not so easy to deal with the opposing party coming to power. It is easy to win well, but it is very difficult to concede defeat gracefully. Winning and losing are both part of the back and forth of the political process, as of so much else in life, and there is maturity in being able to deal with both.

In the business world, most companies that end up failing do just fine during the growth part of the life cycle. Where most companies crash is during the phase where growth slows down, a period that should be a consolidation phase. The typical failing response is to project the early phase of growth and expansion forward into an indefinite future, expecting that growth to continue. Then, when growth slows down, there is an increasing mismatch between expanding output and inventory, and the market for that output. This becomes a setup for a business collapsing like an over-inflated balloon.

In mathematical terms, that is taking a short term trend and extrapolating it forward as a straight line, assuming it will continue to move in the same direction indefinitely. That is why we see so many dire predictions about what will happen in the near future if we don't immediately change our ways. I have seen more than my share of apocalyptic predictions in my lifetime on how civilization will end in x years if we don't start doing y immediately. There are some of those in the news headlines today as I write this, featuring terrified young people who are sure the world will end in ten years if we don't do something now.

Instead, life goes on.

> It was the best of times, it was the worst of times, it was the age of wisdom, it was the age of foolishness, it was the epoch of belief, it was the epoch of incredulity, it was the season of Light, it was the season of Darkness, it was the spring of hope, it was the winter of despair, we had everything before us, we had nothing before us, we were all going direct to Heaven, we were all going direct the other way—in short, the period was so far like the present period, that some of its

> noisiest authorities insisted on its being received, for good or for evil, in the superlative degree of comparison only.
> - Charles Dickens

There is a real wisdom that comes with recognizing and dealing with whole cycles and phases. That comes with time, with perspective, with seeing the whole process - with Saturn sorts of growth in perception.

Cycles of Reincarnation

There is an interesting irony in the model of modern astrology and popular spirituality. The popular notion of multiple lives and reincarnation has eastern philosophical roots, mostly by way of their influence through Theosophy. What is interesting is that the typical concept today is of an ever improving series of lives, progress writ large across multiple lifetimes. This is reincarnation plus evolution.

The actual Eastern system of reincarnation is not progressive or evolutionary at all. It is all about cycles, enormous cycles through mind-boggling lengths of time. Karma is a *wheel* that ultimately just revolves and goes nowhere. The Buddha's answer to that wheel of karma and suffering is not to improve things, but to get off the wheel. Philosophically it is very nearly the direct negation of the modern notion of perpetual progress and expansion.

The concept of reincarnation as evolutionary progress is also very different from the Western model of reincarnation spelled out in the Platonic Myth of Er from the final chapter of Plato's Republic. (I include a long essay on that chapter and its meaning in the appendix to this book.) In Plato's model the lives tend to alternate, with positive lives typically being abused and leading to periods of correction between lives, while difficult or negative lives typically bring about positive responses that lead to periods of rest and reward between lives. It is back and forth, up and down, with no simple linear progress. The progression between lives is itself cyclic. If there is an ongoing growth it is slow, with many ups and downs

Balance

Here the notion of Saturn as awareness of cycles comes in.

What goes up must come down
Spinning wheel spinning round

It is a treadmill, a threshing floor, and also a mill that grinds wheat between revolving stones - millstones that grind slowly but grind exceeding fine.

It is also the great rhythmic and cyclic BREATH where expansion is followed by contraction, in breath by out breath. Growth is followed by decline, and cultures typically have a much easier time dealing with the growth part of a cycle than dealing with the decline part, which typically is reacted to with confusion, disbelief and denial. Look around.

Objectivity

This awareness of cycles is related to a stance of objectivity, being able to stand back from one's current age and critique it. There is a great weakness in valuing only the new, the current, the fashionable. Such a stance gives you no outside perspective from which to become aware of the unbalances and blind spots of the current fads. This is where a sense of history and of entire cycles is so important and is also related to a sense of objectivity.

You can see that this also ties in with other Saturnian themes. Cyclic & historic awareness is connected with accepting changes of fortune, accepting ephemerality, accepting the inevitability of decline and death. Saturn and historical awareness also is related to the meaning of opposition. Objectivity is standing over against the current day's fads to get perspective.

Tradition

One of my main goals in writing this book is to critique the modern bias in our culture against preserving tradition, the tendency to always favor the new over the old. This leads to a horrible loss of very rich and valuable resources. It impoverishes the lives of those who brush off tradition too lightly, as they lose all chance of learning from it.

The general attitude throughout most of astrology's history has been one of respect for tradition. The body of traditional teaching is viewed as a valuable work to be passed down and to be learned from. We have seen how very different this traditional attitude is from our modern world which so highly values progress and the new over the old. Our world is very much future oriented, assuming that old means outmoded, and that old truths are superseded by new truths.

This difference in attitude causes communication problems between traditional and modern astrologers, since they are using very different frames of reference, likely without being conscious of it. On the one hand, a traditional astrologer who values the old would find a problem with modern astrology innovating too quickly, or discarding traditional meanings without thoroughly understanding them first. On the other hand, a modern astrologer, coming from a different point of view, sees the traditional astrologer as afraid of change and innovation, and stuck in the past.

Our attitude towards tradition is related to our attitude towards time, and these are very Saturnine sorts of issues. To learn from Saturn we need to learn from time, from history, from tradition. It is worth paying attention to tradition and not discarding it lightly. There is a reason that this body of teaching has been passed down essentially unchanged for generations. People have repeatedly found it valuable, and it has stood the test of time.

This positive attitude towards tradition shows respect for the intelligence and judgment of the generations that have gone before, and I sometimes find that respect lacking in modern attitudes. As a

Tradition

traditional astrologer I confess it hurts when I see modern books talking about "sweeping away the cobwebs of medieval superstition" when that medieval superstition is the style of astrology I practice. I do not know if that attitude is deliberately condescending, but it definitely comes across as condescending, and as having a peculiarly modern sort of arrogance.

Another one of the good things about valuing tradition is that it gives you something to look up to. In our modern world, with its emphasis on progress and the future, you don't look up, you look out to expand. With such an attitude there is no standard greater than yourself to be a corrective to your current thoughts of the moment. You need a sense of history and tradition to be able to stand back from the modern world's current fads and get a sense of perspective on them.

There are distinctly Saturnian virtues at play here. Tradition passes on the material which stands the test of time, and time is very good at sorting out what is worthy from what is worthless. Going a bit deeper than that, given the thesis that there are eternal laws and structures that we are attempting to apprehend or model from the eternal to the temporal, then that which stands the test of time and tradition most likely corresponds with those eternal laws. This material survives precisely because it has real value.

Hopefully we are at a point in the world of astrology that we can start to look at integrating and synthesizing the best of modern and traditional. One of our tasks today is to see what of modern astrology, the astrology of the 20th century, is likely to stand the test of time.

I propose that a useful test of the value of modern astrology features would be to consider how the new feature interacts with the existing tradition. Does a new feature build on, extend, or shed further light on the tradition? Or does it diminish it, ignore it, contradict it? We can now look at the best of traditional and modern astrology dialoging and learning from each other.

Uranus and Saturn

Earlier I laid out a passage I called the Chesterton Test, restating concept or vague phrases in simple concrete words of one or two syllables. This is another test from the same the same great writer and thinker, that I have seen referred to as,

Chesterton's Fence

"In the matter of reforming things, as distinct from deforming them, there is one plain and simple principle; a principle which will probably be called a paradox.

There exists in such a case a certain institution or law; let us say, for the sake of simplicity, a fence or gate erected across a road. The more modern type of reformer goes gaily up to it and says, 'I don't see the use of this; let us clear it away.'

To which the more intelligent type of reformer will do well to answer: 'If you don't see the use of it I won't let you clear it away.' 'Go away and think. Then, when you can come back and tell me you do see the use of it, I may allow you to destroy it.'"

This paradox rests on the most elementary common sense.

The gate or fence did not grow there. It was not set up by somnambulists who built it in their sleep. It is highly improbable that it was put there by escaped lunatics who were for some reason loose in the street.

Some person had some reason for thinking it would be a good thing for somebody. And until we know what the reason was, we really cannot judge whether the reason was reasonable. It is extremely probable that we have overlooked some whole aspect of the question, if something set up by human beings like ourselves seems to be entirely meaningless and mysterious.

There are reformers who get over this difficulty by assuming that all their fathers were fools; but if that be so, we can only say that folly appears to be a hereditary disease. But the truth is that nobody has any business to destroy a social institution until he has really seen it as an historical institution.

If he knows how it arose, and what purposes it was supposed to serve, he may really be able to say that they were bad purposes, that they have since become bad purposes, or that they are purposes which are no longer served. But if he simply stares at the thing as a senseless monstrosity that has somehow sprung up in his path, it is he and not the traditionalist who is suffering from an illusion."
- GK Chesterton

In these essays I have been quite critical of the usual stereotyped description of Uranus and Saturn as signifying the enlightened youth smashing through old and outmoded structures. This has been a cliche of our culture for well over a hundred years. Orthodoxy is out of fashion, and heresy and rebellion have been the trend since at least the late 1800's. The idea that the new is better than the old, is now an old idea, a mental rut.

Here within our mutable world no structure is absolute and no finite form lasts forever. No country lasts forever, no organization lasts forever. All structures in the material world eventually fall apart.

This means that no earthly religious structure has an eternal monopoly on the entire truth. No earthly church can ever completely embody and contain the one true church. The challenge of any church tradition is to walk the fine line between being the guardians of a tradition of truths that have been passed down, whil avoiding thinking of themselves as the only guardians of the only complete, final and infallible truth. Any structure we build can only point to truth without completely containing it.

This also means that traditional astrology is not better just because it is traditional. The oldest texts are not by definition superior just because they are oldest. Are they worth respecting and learning from? Goodness, yes. Do they contain much of value, even of divinely inspired and eternal value? I am convinced that is true. Are the earliest texts complete and definitive for all time? No.

That is one side of the question.

On the opposite side, there is the danger of thinking that any system is outmoded and ready to be destroyed just because it is old, and that the new is better by definition just because it is new. There is also the danger of thinking that an old structure that is ready to be destroyed has nothing of value in it to be preserved.

Saturn is not always the bad guy, and Uranus is not always the good guy.

Uranus destroys and disrupts outmoded forms, but it also destroys and disrupts things of beauty and value and usefulness. Bombs don't discriminate between good and bad people, they just blow up. Lightning strikes don't choose their targets on the grounds of usefulness or value.

The other side of Uranus, the psychological effect, is that it can manifest as an extreme individualism, a stance of rebellion over against any authority just because it is authority.

The danger of the outer planets is just that - they are outer, beyond the bounds of our usual reality. There is a danger with personally identifying with them, and it is the danger of hubris, ego inflation.

Uranus does seem to have a connection with, and a particular attraction for, the young and with innovation - and this tendency of inflated importance, to think the new is better and more important

Uranus and Saturn

than it really is just because it is new, is a characteristic failing of youth, one that can be a source of serious unbalance. It is also a characteristic failing of our youth-oriented culture as a whole.

In an extreme example, an obsession with Uranus could play out as a self-righteous terrorist hurling a bomb to destroy a massive building - and, in the process, killing hundreds of people and destroying priceless books and art works. It can be disruption for the sake of disruption, rebellion for the sake of rebellion.

All three of the modern outer planets, Uranus, Neptune and Pluto, have this danger of obsession and ego inflation if you identify with them too personally and closely. They are not bound by the usual limits of human personality. Identifying with them has the same kind of hazard as identifying with a god or angel, and you mistaking the god's power for your own. You can get caught up in imagining you have become a god yourself, while in actuality you are the puppet of a low level demon that feeds off of human emotion and desire.

All of the outer planets can be intoxicating and exhilarating. All of the outer planets can give the sensation of being carried beyond the limits of the usual human personality. They can make you feel powerful, invincible, boundless, spiritual, enlightened, infinite, immortal. That is their attraction, that is their fascination, and that is their danger.

Humanity did not immediately become more evolved when Uranus, Neptune and Pluto were discovered, any more than humanity immediately became more mature and responsible when the atomic bomb was invented.

The modern planets do seem to have effects, but they are on another level, and they can work on us in manifestation only by acting through the traditional seven. I like the description of my friend and teacher Ben Dykes - they are not quite planets, but they are something more than fixed stars, and are worth paying attention to if they are in close alignment with a traditional planet. Limiting ourselves to the traditional planets reminds us that we need to respect the limits of human life here on earth in the mutable reality of time and space.

Uranus and Saturn

That is why, as a traditional astrologer, I draw the line of the structure of the solar system with the traditional seven planets. The traditional order of the astrology cosmos was passed down essentially unchanged for over two thousand years. I do not discard such a tradition lightly, and part of the purpose of this book is to re-think that tradition in ways that are relatable to us in the modern world in the context of modern scientific findings about the solar system.

In Chesterton's terms, that fence was put there for a reason. I think I understand that reason, and I wish to preserve the best of that reason here.

When you fall into the stereotyped attitude that new is better than old by definition - and our culture very heavily leans in that direction - there is a danger of thoughtlessly discarding aspects of the tradition that have real value, in the name of change and progress.

Youth can benefit by learning from the accumulated wisdom of tradition. There is a reason some things were passed down for hundreds or thousands of years as having value. This is accumulated experience, this is material that generation after generation has tested and found precious. To discard that lightly is the characteristic hubris of youth.

Today, in our youth oriented culture, it is the role of Saturn to stand back, in an objective position, outside of the fad of the moment, and advise caution. When the message of modern astrology aligns too completely and closely with the current fad - when we think of astrology as a tool for social change and identify it with the latest popular political platform - Saturn is there to give a warning.

This too shall pass.

Saturn and Pluto

Introducing the 3 modern planets, Uranus, Neptune and Pluto, to the system of astrology, did much more than just adding 3 new members to the family. It also drastically changed the meanings of the traditional 7 planets.

The outer planets have taken some of their meanings away from the traditional Sacred Seven planets. In the process, the meanings of the traditional seven have become less rich and complex, thinned down, less multi-dimensional. Part of this thinning down of meaning comes from a modern tendency to want to streamline and conceptualize the meanings of the planets. You often see that each planet is given a single core keyword or concept as a way to grasp its meaning. This is done even by some teachers of traditional astrology.

In the older texts the meanings of the planets are broader, more concrete, and much, much messier - I'm tempted to call them anecdotal. For instance, instead of modern astrology saying that Saturn signifies where you have fear, a traditional text would list how Saturn is associated with graveyards, dark places, underground, the skin, the bones and teeth, old people, diseases like arthritis, the color black, winter, and so on. The meaning of Saturn is given as a set of concrete associations or specific contextual meaning, and you have to feel your way into how these different items all fit together. Starting with concepts rather than concrete associations tends to thin out the process and the meaning.

In addition to becoming more abstract and one-dimensional, some of the meanings originally associated with the traditional planets were transferred to the modern outer planets, which in turn led to a loss of richness of meaning.

To illustrate this, I want to look at how many of the meanings now associated with Pluto were originally associated with Saturn.

Saturn and Pluto

First, let's list some of the common concepts and keywords that are associated with Pluto.

- death
- transformation
- a compulsive pressure to change
- destroying old forms so that new forms can be born
- a need to let go of old things
- pressure
- a process of transformation over time - sheer passage of time is part of the Plutonian pressure

Every one of those meanings was originally associated with Saturn. Let us consider that further.

Saturn is death. The figure of death, a very old person or a skeleton, in a loose black hooded robe, carrying a scythe for the harvest, is a symbol of Saturn. Saturn is skeleton, bones, teeth. Saturn is old people. The scythe is part of the symbolism of death as a harvest.

Saturn is Kronos, Father Time, representing the limitations and structure of a life within material reality and over time. Saturn is the effects of time.

In older texts Saturn is associated with places underground, with death, and with the realm of death, the underworld, which is precisely how we think of Pluto, lord of death and the underworld.

Saturn transits are notorious for applying pressure for change. It is a tester, and any structure that is poorly built or is past its pull date will be destroyed and transformed. Think about your Saturn return! It is precisely that sort of pressure to change that we now associate with Pluto.

Saturn and Pluto

There is also a sort of ruthless pressure of honesty with Saturn transits. You can't get away with any pretense or sham, and you are stripped down to the core essentials and tried. It illuminates your weak points, your vulnerabilities, and that is where you are driven to change. If you work with the change it can be gradual growth. If you resist or ignore the change it can be abrupt, cataclysmic. Things break under the relentless pressure of Saturn.

Now take that previous paragraph and re-read it, substituting Pluto for Saturn. You would not need to change a single word.

I want to look at another way that the modern meaning of Saturn has been simplified and made one-dimensional, to provide a contrast or foil to the outer planets. In modern astrology Saturn is often associated with the status quo, with existing structures, and with resisting change.

However, Saturn also signifies the process of change over time. Saturn is indeed old structures and old patterns - and yet, being time, Saturn is also the pressure for change, that which breaks down old patterns to make way for the new. Saturn is the bones, and the pressure of age that breaks bones. Saturn is also the decaying process. In older texts Saturn is associated with things that are rotting.

Modern astrology often sets up a dichotomy, with Saturn on the one side as the status quo, resisting change, and the outer planets as the forces for change and revolution. We saw that explicitly stated in some of the modern astrologers we looked at. It is a false dichotomy, and it comes from a thinned out, one sided interpretation of the meaning of Saturn.

In modern astrology a Saturn-Pluto aspect might be interpreted as Saturn being the forces resisting change, and Pluto being the forces of irresistible transformation. It is one against the other. This sets up a good-evil dualism where Saturn is the Bad Guy standing in the way of change, while the modern outer planets Uranus through Pluto are the Good Guys, the forces for the new, for revolution and enlightenment.

Saturn and Pluto

Part of the effect of Saturn is precisely the applying of pressure on something that needs to experience change. By separating that dimension of meaning from Saturn we have split a complex process into opposing, less complex opposite forces. We have set up a false dichotomy.

Change is a very complex and mixed process, and keeping the complexity of the traditional meaning of Saturn helps us realize that. Change is not always positive or desirable and along with a seemingly positive change much can be lost or destroyed. It helps us here to remember that life does not come in the form of a straight line march of growth and evolution. It has peaks and valleys, ups and downs, things which survive and things which fall apart.

The traditional meaning of Saturn embodies much of the complexity of the meaning of time and change. Think of the scythe again, symbol of the harvest, of separating the wheat from the chaff. This is a process of weeding and of testing, keeping the valuable and discarding what is worthless. That scythe is one of the key symbols of Saturn as the forces of change and of growth through change, for often what is harvested there is a change of awareness.

It is worth the time to reclaim more of the richness and complexity of the traditional meaning of the Sacred Seven planets. They are, and always will be, the core of our astrology.

Benefic and Malefic

In traditional astrology Saturn is considered the Greater Malefic. To understand malefic we need to look at it with its partner concept benefic. This will draw on and tie together some of the key concepts we have already examined.

The objection to using the concept malefic is part of the curious unbalance of our modern culture that we have repeatedly noted. The modern objections to malefic include some of the following arguments.

First, modern astrologers claim that no planet is completely bad, while traditional astrologers view Saturn as completely evil, and Malefic as meaning only bad. We saw this claim made by Liz Greene, and you will see similar statements made by Stephen Arroyo and other modern humanistic astrologers. We have already established that this position is a caricature of traditional astrology, and we have repeatedly seen that the meanings of Saturn in traditional astrology are very complex and mixed.

Much of modern astrology has a hard time really owning that anything in astrology, or in human life in general, can be labeled as harmful. There is a drive amounting to an obsession to find a positive interpretation for everything in the chart. The motive for this is rooted in the belief in the general power of thoughts to create reality. The danger of labeling an event negative or harmful is that of self-fulfilling prophecy, the fear that if you point to anything negative in their chart then a person will develop a negative mindset, think negative thoughts about it, and thus cause it to manifest.

In the world of positive thinking, which I was raised in, I came to label this The Overwhelming Power of Negative Thinking, and it is part of the dark and ugly shadow of any positive thinking philosophy. There is a sort of terror of having negative thoughts about anything to do with our lives, in the fear that the very act of entertaining them will help to guarantee that these negative things come to pass. (I can recall a self-help book with the title, *You Can't Afford the Luxury of a Negative*

Benefic and Malefic

Thought.) This can create a situation where you become afraid of your own natural thoughts and feelings, creating all sorts of internal knots and problems.

It is impossible to have a world that is completely positive without negative. Period. The belief that human thought is this almighty and powerful is really a kind of overwhelming hubris, human pride. The truth is that human thought is just not omnipotent.

This positive thinking mindset reflects our cultural mania about keeping a positive attitude. This is tied in with our Western culture experiencing an amazing streak of growth and prosperity over the past few centuries. The roots of positive thinking philosophy go back to the late 1800's, the center of an era of unprecedented scientific and technical growth and expansion.

This experience of continued growth has been gradually shifting in the past half century to its opposite, a period of cultural decline, but the shift in actual conditions has not yet been matched by a shift in attitude. We are still thinking like a young growing culture even though that no longer matches the reality around us, and it hasn't matched it for quite awhile now. There has been a lag between the change of conditions and a change of attitude, but I think we are reaching a crisis point in awareness that forces a shift in attitude.

We need to get our balance back.

We've lost the whole notion of balance, of opposites, and we need to recover that to sanely negotiate the reality around us today. The concepts of benefic and malefic are among the core sets of opposites that astrology is built upon, along with day and night, masculine and feminine, active and passive, and many other pairs.

A benefic builds up, grows, is pleasant, builds, expands, pulls things together. A malefic tears down, withers, shrinks or decays, is often unpleasant, tears down, contracts, pulls things apart. Consider them together in this way and it is obvious that they are balancing opposites, and they are also different phases of a complete cycle. Allowing for

Benefic and Malefic

both benefic and malefic brings balance back into the world. We experience both, and both are necessary. Having one without the other would be like perpetually inhaling without ever exhaling, having day without night, having summer without winter.

We can see that benefic and malefic are related to the concept of balance we have already talked about. In our culture it is an ideal to be perfectly successful positive, rich, strong, ever young, and so on. In a more mature world view, an ideal of balance emphasizes developing resilience, the ability to deal with any kind of swing of fortune.

In our world good things happen, and bad things happen. Sometimes you're healthy, sometimes you're sick. Some people seem to be blessed with good health, others have a string of health problems and suffering. This also varies by period in our individual lives. There are good streaks and bad streaks, streaks of health and illness, streaks of joy and of sorrow, streaks of pleasure and suffering. To everything there is a season.

Our culture has largely lost the sense that ups and downs are all a natural, necessary and desirable part of life. We forget that it is often the down and difficult periods where we reap some of the most important long-term rewards. This is part of what I now think of as the paradox of good and bad luck; when we consider their long term effect on our character, often bad luck can help us grow, while too much good luck can weaken and corrupt us both physically and morally.

You can see that the concepts benefic and malefic are related to some other important concepts that we need to consider. These include the concept of fortune, and also how we deal with evil.

All of these concepts intertwine. Given how our minds work we need to examine the concepts in detail separately while remembering that they are part of an interrelated net of ideas.

Evil

No-one wants to touch this topic, including me. I don't claim to have the answers to the problem of Evil when the greatest minds and hearts of history have wrestled with this question for thousands of years. I can only speak from my own mind, and my own heart.

I want to start by sorting out the different meanings of the term.

There is evil in the sense of unfortunate, a happening that causes harm. In this sense, cancer is evil, and a tornado that destroys a house is evil. There is also moral evil, deliberate harm chosen by free will, with intent to cause harm. That is a far darker and more complex problem. As humans we have free will. We can choose, and that means there is always the possibility of choosing to cause deliberate harm.

There are many ways to try and explain why something evil happens to a person. These explanations can also be applied to evil just in the sense of bad fortune, but I want to use the more extreme case of moral evil here.

One way to explain evil is to appeal to a moral law of karma or retribution, that if something bad happens to you it is a reaction or payback for something you did earlier, either in this life or in a previous life. This is a fairly popular modern explanation, and at least at first glance it does seem to offer a reasonable answer. However, the more I think about this option, the less satisfactory I find it. It is an explanation that doesn't really explain anything; it just kicks the can down the road, and holds the person experiencing evil responsible for it from a realm of experience outside of their conscious experience, a realm where they have no memory and no control. It is the equivalent of bluntly saying that whenever anything bad happens to you it is your own fault, you deserved it.

You can see that can be easily abused. A woman was violently raped? It must have been her own fault - blame the victim.

Evil

There is some truth to the popular notion of karma, that how we live our lives does have consequences in further experiences we have, either in this life or after death or in other lives. Useful as that can be, there are serious limitations to using karma to explain malefic events too easily.

Another approach to explaining evil that you will find in some modern astrology, is to view an event as 'evolutionary necessity', meaning that evil suffered is necessary for continued soul growth and evolution, that in some way it is good for you.

If you subscribe to the mind control theory that says you create your own reality, then anything that happens to you is by definition your own fault, and you are seeing your own thoughts mirrored back to you in events. We saw this explicitly stated in the words of several of the modern astrologers we looked at, most notably Liz Greene and Isabel Hickey. It is a very common belief underlying much modern, new age style spirituality.

Yet another approach that has some appeal today that has roots in eastern philosophy is to say that all apparent evil events are just Maya, appearance, illusion, and that behind this appearance there is an unchanging eternal good. This streak is quite also strong in modern astrology as is the mind creation approach, and I think it is common to see a combination of these two approaches together.

Another approach is to appeal to Fortune, which is just that things happen. You happened to be in the room when a gunman walked in and opened fire. This is just bad luck. It doesn't really explain or justify anything, but it has the advantage of not blaming you for something bad happening to you. This approach says that evil things can happen to good people, and it stops there. At first glance this seems the least satisfactory - Liz Greene flat out called it useless - but the more I think of it, the more I think that acknowledging an element of Fortune without assigning blame is very true to human experience. It is an approach that I find can be very practical and useful in the context of actual client work, as it avoids the trap of blaming the person for

Evil

anything bad that happens to them. Dealing with harm is bad enough without an extra burden of guilt tacked on top of that.

Evil can also be justified by claiming that everything works together for good in the end. This appears in the Christian New Testament, in the letters of Paul - *Everything works together for good, for those who love God, according to his purpose.* That is a satisfying explanation if you live in the context of belief in a benevolent creator God, but it can sound like a platitude if you are outside of that framework. It really doesn't explain anything, and at best it is a statement of reassurance that, somehow, all will work out for the best. I would not use that with a client unless I knew they believed in such a God, and even there I would tread very carefully.

Another larger framework for explaining evil is to appeal to Providence, to claim that there is a power and order in the world that can bring good out of evil. This is not quite the same as saying everything works together for good, which sounds too much like saying that evil was part of a plan to bring good from it. Providence says that, even if evil events happen, there is a power in the universe that can bring good out of it. This is the framework that I personally find the most satisfying, but again I would use it with great caution in client readings depending on the person's own beliefs and attitude.

There is reaction that I think is useful regardless of which of these explanations you favor. When something bad, something malefic, even something evil, happens to you, you may have little or no control over that. Admitting that is a first step to dealing well with an evil event. The one area where you do have control and choice is in how you respond. Where do you go from here, and how can you choose your reaction? That is always worthwhile to focus on.

I want to use the Chesterton Test here, restating these in simple words, to really, starkly get us to pay attention to how these various explanations of evil might work out in an actual example.

Gabrielle Giffords is an American politician who was a member of the House of Representatives. On January 8, 2011 congresswoman

Evil

Giffords was the victim of an assassination attempt and was shot point blank in the back of the head. This is evil in both senses of the term; it is extreme harm, and it came from a deliberate intent to harm.

I want to take each of these approaches to dealing with evil and restate them simply and bluntly. Consider each of these responses to that event, in the heat of the moment. I phrase these as first person, but you can also imagine something like these words being said to her husband Mike Kelly standing there next to his wife. Or, you can imagine these being spoken to her after she became conscious again and began to recover.

Karma - "You were shot in the head. It was your own fault."

Create your own Reality - "You were shot in the head. You caused it by your negative thoughts."

Maya - "You were shot in the head. This is not real. The real you cannot be harmed."

Evolutionary Necessity - "You were shot in the head. You need this to grow, it is good for you."

All things lead to good in the end - "You were shot in the head. It will all work out for the best."

Providence - "You were shot in the head. God can bring good out of this."

Fortune - "You were shot in the head. This is not your fault; bad things happen."

The only one of these answers that I find at all emotionally acceptable in the heat of the moment is that of Fortune. It is the one explanation that does not attempt to explain or to give a reason, it just acknowledges that something bad happened and the person is not to blame. Every one of the other responses is attempting to explain the unexplainable, to justify the unjustifiable, to think of the unthinkable.

Evil

Evil, real moral evil, is a violation, a contradiction, something that should not ever happen. But it does. We have to start there.

In the history of religion and theology there are several classic arguments for the existence of God, and there are also arguments against God's existence. I find some of the arguments for God's existence to be very compelling if I think them through.

Coming at it from the other side, as far as I am concerned there is really only one argument against the existence of a good creator God which has any real weight, and that is the existence of moral evil in the world. Given that God is good and creation is good, how do you explain the existence of moral evil? Faced with an actual evil event I do not know of any argument that doesn't sound like mere juggling of words.

Any approach to evil has to begin by squarely facing the stark horror and contradiction of it. We can't explain it away. We have to have plain acceptance before we can do anything else. "You were shot in the head. I am here with you." Or, better yet, just hold them. Just be there. We need to start with plain naked acceptance before we can extend sympathy or aid.

Humans have free will, the ability to choose. That necessarily includes the freedom to choose evil. Since we interact here on earth this means that any person can be on the receiving end of someone else's evil act. The only way I can think of to answer the argument against God's existence because of evil is to argue that the good of human free will outweighs the possibility of evil that necessarily comes with it.

This leads to a higher level question. Given that evil acts can be chosen and can happen, does the order of the universe work in such a way that good can come out of that?

Can good come out of evil?

I am personally convinced that it can. I think the same horrible example that referred to earlier, the shooting of American Congresswoman Gabrielle Giffords, is a very good argument for that. I think she is doing important and meaningful work now, and I admire the strength and integrity of both her and her husband Mark Kelly.

Ultimately, the only answer to evil that I personally find satisfying at all is the belief in Providence, that there is some underlying power in our universe that is able to bring good even out of the worst evil. This is also a testimony to something powerful and resilient in the human spirit that can respond in this way, and ultimately I think we have to trace that to the power which creates and sustains the human spirit.

This is not making the evil good in the first place, or saying that it is part of God's plan, or explaining it away, or saying that everything works out for the best in the long run. It is more like a miraculous kind of alchemy or transformation. Evil is not planned, but it can be transformed to bear good fruit.

Eventually.

But even with my belief in Providence, I do not feel I can push that on anyone else. I think that each individual person has to face that ultimate question in the privacy and solitude of their own soul and come to their own decision.

Faced with a person who is dealing with the great harm of an evil action, I would not start speaking of God's Providence. If they do not share my faith there, it would be an affront to push it on them. It could easily feel too much like explaining it away. Faced with actual evil, the best we can do is to try to find the courage and integrity to face the stark horror of it without explaining it away. That, and be ready to offer love and aid in whatever way we can.

Evil and Transformation

There is another interesting phenomenon that sometimes happens with facing evil. Consider these examples.

There is Victor Frankl, the Jewish psychologist who was a victim of the Nazi death camps during World War Two, who survived and eventually wrote *Man's Search for Meaning*, one of the great books of the 20th century, a tribute to the resilience and greatness of the human spirit.

There is Fyodor Dostoyevsky, who came to his belief in the Christian God from the experience of being sentenced to death, and then reprieved.

There is Alexandr Solzhenitzyn, who experienced the Russian labor camps and later wrote *The Gulag Archipelago*. Solzhenitzyn is East Orthodox Christian.

There is Anwar Sadat, former President of Egypt, who was a violent radical until he experienced being arrested and thrown in solitary confinement in horrific conditions - and then emerged with a new sense of faith, and became a non-violent pioneer for peace in the Middle East until he was assassinated.

In our current day there is Jordan Peterson, who credits the motivation for his work on the goodness of the human spirit to the experience of coming face to face with the existence of real evil, and the empty horror if the world stopped there and there was no force for good.

All of these people came face to face with the raw, stark experience and realization of naked moral evil - and all emerged with a strong faith in ultimate good.

We are face to face with a mystery here. I have not walked that path, so I can only point to it and acknowledge it without attempting to explain it. Sometimes we need to stare into the abyss of human Evil in order to really understand what The Good means.

Fortune

I want to begin this essay on Fortune with a long quote from C S Lewis from a book called *The Discarded Image: An Introduction to Medieval and Renaissance Literature*. This is an excellent book to give a feel for what it must have been like to live within the traditional world where the spheres of astrology were a given part of the natural world order. The Dante quote Lewis refers to is from the *Commedia*.

> We have already seen that all below the Moon is mutable and contingent. We have also seen that each of the celestial spheres is guided by an Intelligence. Since Earth does not move and therefore needs no guidance, it was not generally felt that an Intelligence need be assigned to her.
>
> It was left, so far as I know, for Dante to make the brilliant suggestion that she has one after all, and that this terrestrial Intelligence is none other than Fortune. Fortune, to be sure, does not steer the Earth through an orbit; she fulfills the office of an Intelligence in the mode proper to a stationary globe.
>
> God, says Dante, who gave the heavens their guides 'so that every part communicates splendour to every other, equitably distributing light, likewise ordained a general minister and guide to worldly splendours; one who should from time to time transfer these deceptive benefits from one nation or stock to another in a fashion which no human wisdom can prevent. That is why one people rules while another grows weak.'
>
> For this she is much abused by mortal tongues, 'but she is blessed and never hears them. Happy among the other primal creatures, she turns her sphere and rejoices in her bliss.'

Fortune

> ...Since worldly splendours are deceptive, it is fit that they should circulate. The pond must be continually stirred or it will become pestilential. The angel who stirs it rejoices in this action as the heavenly spheres rejoice in theirs.
>
> The conception that the rise and fall of empires depends not on desert, nor on any 'trend' in the total evolution of humanity, but simply on the rough justice of Fortune, giving all their turns, did not pass away with the Middle Ages.

This is a very rich passage, one that is very different from our modern way of thinking about the world. I think it raises some very worthwhile points, and I want to approach it here from a couple of different directions.

The model of fortune which Lewis describes here fits in the traditional world model where the disordered area is within the moon's orbit, the sublunary world, the world of the four elements. Outside of that sphere is the realm of the seven classical planets where the movement is very regular and predictable. We have ephemerides of the planetary positions for thousands of years into the past and future, and by comparison the world here on earth is disorderly and unpredictable mess. We can predict the positions of planets thousands of years in advance, and we can't accurately predict the weather a few days out.

Part of the implicit purpose of Fortune in this model is to help us realize that appearances are deceptive down here in the mutable world. The purpose of changes of fortune is to teach what is really valuable. In this model good or bad fortune in the usual worldly sense is not a matter of merit but of luck. That runs totally against the grain of our achievement-oriented society. Fortune takes turns, a concept related to cycles having ups and downs. We need to experience both to have full human lives.

This means that the purpose of life is not related to good or bad fortune in any way. This also means that ultimately we cannot take credit for having fortunate lives, nor can we take blame for having unfortunate

Fortune

lives. We are part of a larger order, and good or bad fortune in that sense is beyond our control.

This is a place where traditional and modern astrology have distinctly different purposes.

We have seen that there is a strong moral streak in 20th century astrology, the message that you get what you deserve. Traditional astrology does not take that approach. In traditional astrology the evaluation tools of dignity and debility tell which way Fortune is trending at the moment, if this will be a good or bad time, easy and fortunate, or difficult and unfortunate. The whole question of moral purpose doesn't come up in the usual traditional context relative to good and bad fortune. In traditional astrology, and in the traditional model of the cosmos, good and bad fortune happen to both good and bad people.

Since a central part of modern astrology is addressing the issue of purpose, for the concept of Fortune to be useful we need to think how it would fit in a larger purpose. As the quote from Dante shows, we need to start by considering what is *not* the purpose of human life - and that eliminates a lot of the purposes we might first assume.

The purpose of life is not to succeed, or to win, or to be rich, or to be wealthy, or strong, or to have any other external quality. The purpose of life is not the fine art of doing whatever you choose, or manifesting your full potential, or imposing your vision on the world. The purpose of life is not to be highly evolved or enlightened. Every one of these purposes I listed are at root elitist, as they can apply only to a chosen few. Just a moment's thought should show that any of those goals as the true purpose of life renders the lives of a large proportion of people throughout history either less valuable or worthless.

If you say the purpose of life is to be wealthy then you have reduced the value of poor people's lives to nothing.

If the purpose of life is to be healthy, then you have to make sense of the lives of people who battle with sickness or weakness all their lives.

Fortune

If the purpose of life is to live long, then you need to explain the lives of people who die young.

If the purpose of life is to be spiritually evolved or awakened, where does this leave the lives of poor and uneducated people who have time and energy only to work hard to make ends meet, and no time for the luxury of spiritual enlightenment.

If all human lives have worth then the purpose of human life cannot be tied to any form of good or bad fortune.

There is another approach from the tradition that we can consider here, one that runs counter to our modern notion of the forward march of evolution and progress.

We mentioned Plato's myth of Er in book 10 of *The Republic*. That chapter is examined in a long essay in the Appendix of this book. If you read the description there of people choosing the Lot of the life they want, it is clear that first appearances can be deceptive. What looks like a life of wealth and power has consequences leading to tyranny, greed and cruelty. What looks like a life of hardship and struggle ends up being satisfying and builds virtue.

Plato also points out in his story that the lives generally tend to alternate. People who are just off of a period where they were rewarded between lives are likely to choose an easy life, with hard consequences calling for punishment after that life. People just off of a period of punishment are more likely to choose a difficult or humble life that will have good fruit and end up being rewarded. In this model people as a general rule do better with the difficult lives than with the positive and easy ones.

This model does not have straight line progress and growth between lives. It bounces, back and forth, up and down.

We are looking at a different sort of standard of values here. In the list of possible life goals we considered - wealth, power, fortune and so on - all of the goals depend on some external fulfillment. In the Platonic model the only real measure of the worth of a life is in terms of virtue. Regardless of the external circumstances of life, the important question is whether a person chooses to consistently act in virtuous ways. Those are the criteria that result in the periods of reward or punishment in the Platonic myth.

I think that part of the reason that many modern people find the notion of Fortune hard to deal with is that our conception of the purpose of human life has changed so very much in the modern world. In our western affluent society we have gotten used to the idea that we deserve good fortune. The media goes a long way towards encouraging that value, as it is a very good motivator to sell things. *Go for it, you deserve it.*

If the purpose of life in our modern world isn't to be successful in any number of ways - rich or strong or beautiful or famous or intelligent - then what is? Can people be born poor, or weak, or deformed, struggle all their lives, and still have lives that have value, that are worth living? Think of the people you know whose lives fit this description - preferably people you care for or admire - and ask yourself: what is it you admire?

My parents were working class, Brooklyn, New York City, of Italian and Irish Catholic ancestry, growing up in an era of serious anti-Catholic bias when shops would display signs saying, *Help Wanted: No Irish Need Apply.*

My mom was a sewing machine operator, my dad was a book-keeper who wanted to join the army during World War Two but was prevented by poor vision. He originally tried memorizing the eye chart to get into the army, but failed on a re-exam when war broke out.

Both of my parents worked very hard, both lived very frugally, both did all they could to give my sister and I a good life. When my sister developed signs of serious mental illness in her teens, both my parents dedicated the latter half of their lives to taking care of her the best they could.

Fortune

Both were intelligent but not brilliant. Neither graduated high school; neither had the chance. They were not perfect parents - I inherited a lot of their problems - but they gave my sister and I what they could.

I think of them as ordinary saints, or good decent people. And, I do not think that people like my parents are uncommon.

Whatever it is that my parents had is what makes human life valuable, and it has nothing to do with good or bad fortune. It also has nothing to do with how spiritually evolved they were. Both had more than their share of bad fortune and suffering, and they were good people, either despite that, or because of that. I now lean towards the latter way of thinking, that their challenges are part of what made them the good people they were.

The older I get, the more I value simply being a good, decent caring ordinary person, and the more I realize how difficult that really is.

There is a streak of modern astrology that is elitist. Here I am deliberately not giving specific names because I am being very critical, and I am trying to make the description vague enough that it can't be tracked back. That elitist streak is implicitly there when you say that the stars govern the actions of the mass of ordinary and unaware people, but that if you aware enough you have the ability to choose what happens to you. And of course, the astrologer and their audience are not among that mass of unaware people, they are among the advanced, the evolved, the spiritually aware.

You will also see the unstated assumption that the astrologer and their audience are at the cutting edge of the spiritual evolution of humanity, lighting a lamp in the darkness of unawareness and leading a path forward for the unenlightened masses. I have heard an astrologer refer to such unevolved people as *cattle*, a comment followed by condescending laughter among the crowd. How fortunate we are to be evolved past that!

Fortune

If the purpose of human life is spiritual evolution, then people who are more evolved lead more valuable lives. The conclusion follows the premise.

That feels horribly wrong to me.

There is something very important I am getting at here. Whatever it is that makes a human life worth living cannot be confined only to the rich, or the famous or successful or strong or whatever. It needs to be some quality that is part of ordinary human life, any human life, rich or poor, known or unknown, healthy or ill. It cannot be something elitist that is confined to the few.

Human life is not all about success. The best words I can find for what is important in life are character and virtue.

Many world spiritual traditions refer to a time of judgment at death, where each person faces the consequences of how their life was lived. It is in Plato, it is in the Bible in Christianity and Judaism, it is in Islam, and also in the Hindu model of reincarnation.

What is being judged at death? Whatever it is, it is the same thing that can make a life that is poor and hard working and short still be a worthwhile thing of beauty and infinite value.

Part of the purpose of Fortune, the role it plays in the whole system of human life, is to teach us what is not important and what is. There is a law worth living by that makes life worthwhile regardless of what Fortune throws at you. Precisely that may be part of the purpose of Fortune in the overall order.

We live within a larger order, and we are happier and more fulfilled, more human, when we find a sense of that order and can live within it. Fortune reminds us of that. When our pride and ambition starts to get the better of us, and we think that we deserve all the good things that happen to us, that is when Fortune kicks us in the butt - if we're lucky.

We are raised up by Fortune, and we are brought low. To be brought low, to be cast down, is to be humiliated, to be humbled; the two words have the same root meaning. Humility is a peculiarly Saturnian virtue, and one of the most beautiful virtues of all.

This understanding of Fortune also gives us a framework for working with the concepts of benefic and malefic, which is related to the ups and downs of fortune. We need to get past the idea that only fortunate things are supposed to happen. That is not how life works out down here in our mutable sublunary world, and this world would not serve us well if all experienced only good fortune. As humans we need the mix of good and bad, fortunate and unfortunate, difficult and easy, and we benefit from the mix. Our life is in cycles, and we need all phases of the cycle.

In the area of astrology client work this understanding of Fortune helps us get away from the deep seated modern view that you are responsible for your life, and for everything that happens to you. That can have really nasty psychological effects. On top of dealing with blows of bad fortune you would have mixed in feelings of responsibility, guilt, and blame. There can often be the feeling that the person must have done something to deserve this, either in this life or a previous life. That takes an already difficult situation and makes it ten times worse.

I have had client sessions where the central part of the purpose is helping the person realize they were not to blame for whatever kind of serious accident or illness was the core reason for the session.

Once that is out of the way - once we clear away any unnecessary and harmful feelings of guilt and shame about experiencing bad fortune - then we are clear to address how the person can choose their response to the situation. We may not necessarily control what happens to us, but the one thing we can choose is how we wish to respond and deal with it. That is a very powerful Stoic principle that is also good mental and emotional hygiene.

Old Age

In this chapter, I want to share from my own life experience, and touch on some of the things I am learning about aging. Our culture gives me few role models for aging well, so I am having to experiment and explore on my own. I am currently 67 years old, and I think of myself as an entry-level senior citizen. I am having some major health problems this year that have me really feeling my age and my mortality in a new way.

I am think our modern culture's general approach to old age is very limited. The media presents us with pictures that encourage us to pretend that aging just doesn't happen - either that, or rephrase or repackage aging so that it sounds like a continuation of youth.

You're only as old as you feel. 60 is the new 40. 75 years young.

Bull.

I used to subscribe to AARP magazine (AARP is American Association of Retired Persons), and it was filled with photos of smiling, healthy, physically fit, affluent people, on golf courses or next to pools - color in their hair and a spring in their step, ready to enjoy all of that wonderful leisure time.

I don't know any people like the ones I see in those pictures.

This attitude of denying the effects of aging seems to be especially limiting for women, who are encouraged to keep their youthful appearance just as long as possible. In AARP some of the articles about women in entertainment careers take that to a point somewhere between funny and pitiful. If a woman in her seventies is still trying to look and act like she is in her early twenties then something is seriously wrong.

The picture presented implies that old age is all **about me**, about relaxing and enjoying myself. It is a very self-centered sort of attitude.

With all of this artificial self-centered packaging we have lost the sense of old age itself as having its own particular and unique value, different from youth. We have also have lost all sense of the aged having a particular gift to give that can only come with age. We need to get that back.

This ties in with our cultural unbalance that we discussed previously. It fits with our culture's worship of youth and of the new. Anything old is outmoded and to be discarded, and unfortunately that often includes old people. Sadly, it is common to see seniors talked down to or else ignored. As you get older you become increasingly invisible. I am just starting to experience that.

The Special Virtues of Age

The special virtues of old age are woven in with the different qualities of Saturn that I am trying to recover in this book. I want to consider some of those virtues here. I also want to do justice to the particular difficulties of age, the malefic side of the picture, those difficulties you have when things fall apart and quit functioning. Old age has special challenges, and also special gifts, and I don't care to minimize either dimension.

This is particularly difficult today because the worth of this period of life, its particular virtues, are really not recognized in our culture. One of the needs for a sense of meaning in life is to have the feeling that you have something worthwhile to give, to offer, to do for others. In a lot of ways we have robbed older people of that quality and of that opportunity.

I am learning that I have a different kind of thinking and awareness as I get older. It is partly a matter of perspective, of being able to stand back from the immediate moment and consider it from the outside. It also comes from having lived long enough to get a sense of overall cycles, of ideas, fads and fashions coming, growing, peaking and then fading. When you are young it is all too easy to be swept up in the fad or mania of the moment. As you get older it is easier to stand back and

Old Age

get some perspective and distance, to consider the moment's events in the larger context of history.

In order to really practice this virtue, to appreciate this quality of age, you need to allow time and space. You need time to stop, to think, to contemplate. You need time to be alone with your thoughts, and time to do the sorts of mental processing needed to get this perspective.

You cannot do this kind of thinking when the TV is always on, or when you are tethered to your phone or computer. You cannot do this kind of thinking when you keep yourself constantly busy. The senior environments that I have seen work against this sort of quiet time, as they provide constant interruptions and distractions at every moment, with the ubiquitous TV screen always on, and there is often the experience that you are always being watched, an environment like Winston Smith's worst nightmare.

There is a reason why slow, profound, insightful thinking is a Saturnine quality. It is characteristic of old age if you do it right, and it takes time, space and effort to blossom.

Old age is a time when you are staring your own mortality in the face. Quickly or slowly, death is approaching. This is a process that strips you down to the basics, to the important things in life. Growing old, stripping down, getting to the basics, getting to the bare bones, are all Saturnian concepts.

I am finding another quality to be characteristic of the later years. Given that we live in two worlds at once, temporal and eternal, old age is a good period to increasingly withdraw from attachment to temporal concerns and spend more time focusing on what is eternal.

Old age can offer the special opportunity for time to just be quiet and think, to think for its own sake - not time to think in order to plan or do, just time to think in order to understand. It is a good time for tying things together mentally, seeing the whole pattern. This does not happen by accident: it takes intention, it takes time and space, and it takes practice and sustained work.

Old Age

I spend a good amount of time praying now as I am getting older (I am age 67 as of this writing), and I find that prayer takes on a new dimension. I suspect that this is a natural part of aging, as the veil between the worlds gets thinner. I am less attached here, I have less work to do, so I can relax some of the fierce focus on this world and allow my mind to be open in other ways.

Over the past few years it has become increasingly important to me to be praying for the dead, for those who have gone before. Almost all traditional cultures have practices that honor the dead, think about them, make offerings to them and pray for them. I increasingly get the feeling that I need to be praying for the dead. It is an inner need. Tradition teaches us that there are prayers we can offer for the dead that they cannot do for themselves, and that the dead can pray for us and help us in ways we cannot help ourselves.

We have lost something very precious in our modern culture, that sense of a living community with our ancestors. Notice how this subject ties together with our attitude towards time, and history, and tradition, and cycles. All of the concepts intertwine.

Yet another aspect of aging happens because, as I grow old, the world around me is changing also. I find myself getting increasingly out of sync with current fads and styles. This is a theme that shows up in some of the Anne Rice vampire stories. In her world the vampires are theoretically immortal, but can age to the point where they are so out of sync with the world around them that they have the desire to die. Immortality on earth can get old. I sometimes wonder if I will get to a point where I no longer feel at home in the modern world, that I will feel like I don't fit in anymore. I don't mean this in a maudlin or self-pitying sense; the world around me changes in ways that I don't want to fit in with.

I find myself wanting to think about my own death. I do not think this is being morbid, I think it is perfectly normal and natural to do this as one gets older. It is difficult for me to find people to easily and

Old Age

naturally talk about my own death. I suspect I am more at ease with my own aging and death than most of my friends.

There is such a thing as getting to a point where you have lived long enough.

Our medical system, and much of our culture, is obsessed with the idea and practice of extending life as much as possible, taking drastic measures with no regard to quality of life or to cost. That seems to be starting to change now, with my very large Baby Boomer generation getting old and approaching death. I am increasingly seeing movements to raise awareness about quality of death, choosing when and how to die.

Old age does not need to be an enemy. It has its own special treasures to be unlocked, and I am just starting to discover them.

Suffering

Suffering is a natural and expected part of life. It is completely unrealistic to expect to have a life without suffering. If there is suffering in our lives, then we must acknowledge suffering in our astrology. It is not to be glossed over, or minimized; it is to be accepted and dealt with.

There is good evidence that dealing with a certain amount of suffering is a necessary part of growing up and maturing. People who are overly shielded from suffering lack a certain maturity and strength, an ability to deal with adversity when it does come. And, adversity can and will come at any time.

It is the same with pain, and here I am talking about physical pain. Pain is not quite the same thing as suffering, but the two are definitely related. A certain amount of pain, sometimes severe pain, is also a common part of human life. It is only in our affluent and sheltered modern world that we could expect all pain to be treated or banished.

Suffering can have a positive outcome in terms of inner growth if it is dealt with well. I think it is true that part of the purpose of a human life is to experience suffering, that it is not an incidental or unfortunate side-effect. There is something about suffering that cuts very close to the purpose of our life here.

Attitude makes a large difference here, and it is worth studying the great Stoic philosophers, Marcus Aurelius, Epictetus and Seneca, for an education on dealing well with suffering.

Much human suffering is second level suffering, or suffering about suffering, where our reaction to suffering increases it. Thinking of these two levels, we have greatly limited control over suffering, but we have a great deal of choice as to how we respond to suffering, and if our response minimizes it or adds to it.

Suffering

Suffering is a natural part of any process of change and growth. For example, considering how differing phases of suffering fit into the grief process. Going through that suffering well can make grieving powerful and positive; failing to face it can create further blocks and problems.

Redemptive Suffering

There is a another dimension of suffering I want to touch on here. This is the idea that suffering can be redemptive, a voluntary suffering taken on oneself in order to help others. This concept of redemptive voluntary suffering is particularly strong in the Christian religion, especially Roman Catholic, where it is a deep and enduring part of the tradition. When so very many great people have embraced redemptive suffering for thousands of years I assume that there is a good reason for that belief, and I assume it is not just a derangement or a pathology.

This idea that we can suffer to assist each other is in turn related to the idea that we need to pray for each other. There are ways that other people, living or dead, can pray for me that I cannot pray for myself. In the Catholic system this is the communion of Saints, the community of all of us going through time, all who have ever lived or will live, and that we can suffer together, help each other, support each other, and that we have an obligation to pray for each other and to help each other as a human community.

This touches on the mystery of collective suffering, the idea that all of our suffering is linked with each other. We never suffer alone, we always suffer with and for others, and other people's suffering affects all of us at a deep level. Such a belief and practice only makes sense if we do not live separate individual lives, but that our lives make sense and have meaning only in context of a larger whole. All of our lives are connected; none of us lives or dies to ourself alone.

There is a dimension of Catholic prayer practice where a person can offer up their own suffering as a gift or a healing for others. In such a setting there can be an attitude even of welcoming suffering or voluntarily taking it on. This attitude views suffering itself as something positive and beautiful. As I said, I have seen that far too often in the lives of some of the greatest of saints for me to dismiss that as a mere aberration or a pathology.

I do know from my own experience that offering up my own suffering to help others does lighten the suffering and pain. It makes it easier to bear, and gives it a sense of meaning and purpose. Suffering in such a setting is no longer something to avoid or run from.

We should still do all we can to alleviate suffering. Many of the greatest saints like Mother Theresa of Calcutta and Dorothy Day here in America have done just that, usually without drawing any attention to the suffering they undergo themselves.

As we touched on earlier, this uncovers another truth, that the worst of suffering is actually second level, or suffering about suffering. Even dealing with strictly physical pain, you can learn that pain is far worse when you tense up against it and fight it, and that it is easier to bear when relax and breathe into it. Embracing pain makes it easier to bear.

Embracing suffering, and suffering for others, are ways of relaxing and breathing into a mystery of compassion that ties us all together.

Caritas

Finally, I want to touch here on suffering from *Caritas*. The Latin word Caritas has a depth and richness of meaning far greater than any English equivalent. It connotes a depth of selflessness missing in our word love, and it is worlds deeper than the now cheapened English word Charity which has degenerated to mean something like free handouts for the poor.

Caritas is not an emotion but is more like a living force. In religious terms you can think of it as the merciful loving-kindness of the Divine

Suffering

that creates and sustains the universe. The power of Caritas is the power that creates worlds and that binds them together.

When we suffer with Caritas, we open our heart to the suffering of others. We have compassion for a person in the same way that God has compassion for all people, and we join our suffering and our caring to God's. When we suffer through Caritas God has compassion through us. The great mystics of the Christian tradition are unanimous in saying that such compassion and voluntary suffering on our part has a great power for good.

Consider spending time rethinking your attitude towards suffering.

Death

In order to make my point in this chapter I want to tell the story of two deaths that I have experienced personally in my family. One of them was a very ugly and hard death. The second one, nearly thirty years later, was a very beautiful and blessed death. These were two of the most formative events in my entire life, and they went far to shaping my attitude towards being human and mortal and towards death and dying.

Both were deaths from cancer.

In the first, a young relative of mine was diagnosed with melanoma, a deadly form of skin cancer. It was treated and went into remission, and then returned. After the return it took about a year before he died, and during that period it was known that his chances of surviving were very low.

What made this death ugly? He denied and fought that death to the very bitter end - to the last day, as far as I know. In the final days he was cared for at home by his parents, and he died at home. My last memory of him, a few weeks before he died, was there in the family living room, with him little more than a skeleton at this point. And the only words I remember him saying were, *Keep me going. Keep me going.*

The toll on the family, on his parents and all of the relatives, was absolutely brutal. Death was there hanging in the room, so vivid you could smell it - and no-one could say the word, because he wasn't ready to hear it.

When he finally did die, his parents needed to make the arrangements for his burial, and his memorial service, during those first few weeks after his death. No plans had been made. They were very strong and gracious in how they handled it, but the emotional cost must have been brutal.

Death

Keep me going. Keep me going.

The second death was my wife Cindy, who was diagnosed with stage 4 breast cancer. She went through a couple of years of the usual cancer treatment, the debilitating chemotherapy and radiation. There came a point where it became obvious to pretty much everyone at once that the treatment was not working - to Cindy, to me, to her doctor, to my daughter. We all were ready at about the same time to break the news to each other and to say, this isn't working. She's dying.

Cindy and I dealt with that by just accepting the news. We set up home hospice in our living room, and I took care of Cindy during those last three months of her life before she died. During that period we had a steady stream of visitors to our house, of friends and relatives coming to spend time with us. About a month before she died we did a public memorial service for her, while she was still alive, so that she could experience it. That service was a peak day in our lives together, one of the peak days of my entire life. After the service, which included tribute speeches, some belly dancing and a lot of a cappella singing, we had a period at the end where we sang song after song while everyone in the church - hundreds of people, the church was full - got a chance to come up to Cindy and say goodbye.

Cindy was completely surrounded by love and she knew it.

A few days after that service she started rapidly declining, and died in our living room a few weeks later. That last three months of her life was a mountain-top experience for me. It was worth all the rest of our years together just for those last three months.

If I consider the deaths I have seen others experience in my family and community of friends, unfortunately it seems that the first attitude towards death is the more prevalent in our culture. There is the compulsion to fight bravely on, to take every possible measure and every possible expense - and maybe, get around to admitting that death is inevitable maybe a day or two before it occurs. That leaves next to no time for people to say goodbye, make their peace, make their plans and so on.

Death

Think of the number of times you have seen people say that so and so lost their brave battle against cancer, or whatever disease. Death is the enemy to be fought tooth and nail to the last instant.

Keep me going.

Fortunately, as my very large baby boom generation is moving into our final years, I am seeing a significant shift in attitude towards death, and I am seeing more resources dedicated to making death itself positive. People are realizing that a good death can be a wonderful and God-given blessing, a crowning blossom on a life.

Death is Saturn. Fighting or denying Saturn does no good, and just causes more and deeper suffering. Accepting and working with Saturn can produce blessings - hard blessings, yes, but deep and meaningful blessings nonetheless.

Fear of God

Spiritual maturity involves realizing that you are not the center of the universe, that the world doesn't revolve around you, and that you are under the jurisdiction of a greater law and a greater power. You are always standing in the presence of the living Eternal Law.

I think that is the truth to the Fear of God being the beginning of wisdom.

I realize this phrase is out of style. I am attempting to gently approach something very important here that our modern day culture has largely lost sight of.

Your choices matter, your thoughts matter, your actions matter and have consequences. This does not mean that your thoughts control reality. It does mean that your thoughts and actions exist in a larger context, and have consequences in that larger context. This includes realizing that there really are eternal moral laws wired into the structure of the universe, inner and outer, and those same laws are wired into the center of the human heart. This realization needs to be gut level, experiential and emotional to really be effective and life-changing.

There really is an eternal law of justice that is part of how the universe works. If you act in unjust ways, sooner or later they are self-defeating and will catch up to you. This is the main theme of Plato's Republic, and of other great ethical works from traditions all over the world.

There is another realization harder to put into words. It is part idea, part feeling, part deep experience beyond either of those.

Prior to this experience we somehow think that our real innermost thoughts and emotions are hidden from everyone and everything but ourselves. Deep inside of us is the feeling that our thoughts are private, and that no-one outside of ourselves could possibly know what we think and feel in the privacy of our hearts. Along with this is the feeling that we can somehow get away with doing things provided we can keep them hidden. Children act like they have that sense, and it can be amusing to the adults around them. We are all like those children for much of our lives.

If we are very, very fortunate, there comes that beautiful and awesome moment when we realize some important truths.

We realize that we are always seen.

We realize that we are always known.

We realize that there is That within us which knows our every move and every thought.

We realize that every moment of our lives we are held accountable for our every word and deed.

Spiritual traditions all over the world teach that that there will come a time when we must give an account of our lives. There comes a moment we realize that the time when we must give that account - is always right now. That is what I mean by the Fear of God. And the Bible is right, the fear of God is the beginning of wisdom. It is also the end of wisdom, and the source of wisdom, and the doorway to the love of God.

I am a being in time, always standing in the presence of eternity. This is a very Saturnian sort of experience. This, I think, is why Saturn is often related to wisdom in the old texts.

Saturn bridges the worlds of time and eternity, and the very Saturnian experience of the Fear of God brings us much closer to the source of all.

Humility

Humility is a particularly Saturnian virtue, and one that we have largely lost and devalued in our modern culture. For the modern world, pride and self-esteem are far more emphasized and far more important. Humility runs very much against the grain of our modern culture which is all about self-assertion and self-visibility.

With our modern world focused on the fulfillment of our human potential, and of acting out our desires and dreams, worshipping the inner divinity slides very easily over into self-worship. With no higher power above us we exalt individual human worth.

This is where people like Saint Theresa of Avila provide such a very marked contrast. If you have read any of her writing, there is a complete and total self-effacement that sounds like she is giving no value to herself; and yet the woman had an astounding strength, will-power and perseverance.

This points to where humility fits in with the rest of the structure of meaning we have been building. In her own terms, Theresa knew that by herself she could do nothing, but with God she could do all things.

> Let nothing disturb thee,
> Nothing affright thee
> All things are passing;
> God never changeth;
> Patient endurance
> Attaineth to all things;
> Who God possesseth
> In nothing is wanting;
> God alone sufficeth.
> - Theresa of Avila

Theresa realized that we have an internal support from the very structure and reality of the universe itself. It is within us and without

Humility

us. It is at our very core, but also far, far beyond each of us individually, so that there is no risk of mistaking it for our personal selves.

When we align ourselves with the order of the universe, there is no longer the need to place importance on our own individual worth.

Our own individual isolated worth is not what is important, and is not what survives death.

It is when we stand in awareness of the eternal world, in the presence of eternal law, that values like Humility and Mercy and Justice become all important. They point to what is eternal, what is real and survives our temporal experience.

Humility is that wonderful and liberating realization that I as an individual just am not that important. And yet, I as an individual as connected connected to the source have an eternal worth and infinite worth. This realization is most effective when I am able to stop thinking about myself and my own importance and concentrate on my given task at hand, working to the best of my ability without worrying about myself or the outcome of my work. What is important is not me, but the work to be done, the service to be performed.

In some ways humility is my absolute favorite of the virtues, in that it is impossible to claim it for oneself. In the very act of claiming humility for myself I cease to be humble. It is a virtue that must be invisible to itself.

Saturnian humility relates to invisibility and to selfless service. It is the direct opposite of the self-assertion of the Sun. It deals with work done outside of visibility, outside of the public eye, with no credit taken. It is self-effacing and self-erasing. Being lowly, humility has an advantage that pride can never have, an advantage we have largely lost in our modern world.

Pride can only look down; humility can look up.

Final Thoughts

While working on the first draft of this book I had surgery to remove a cancerous tumor. I am still dealing with the aftermath of that now, and I do not know how it will turn out. Being diagnosed with cancer gives the work on the themes of this book a personal and urgent note, and I have tried to share some of that urgency, especially in the essays in part three.

I am resisting the urge to take all the themes of this book and tie them up in a nice neat bow here at the end. Like everything else in astrology, the meanings of Saturn are complex and multi-dimensional, and there is a sort of glorious living sloppiness to it all. Here I want to sum my main purposes for writing this book.

In learning astrology in general, and understanding Saturn in particular, I want to emphasize how very important it is to build on the traditional material. It is not neatly systematized for our modern minds, but there is a wealth of detail and meaning there. I tried to pull out some of the main themes, and I am sure there are more to be found. The historical survey in Part One is a good place to start explore further.

To understand Saturn in the context of traditional astrology we need to be aware of the assumptions and limitations of our modern world view. I have tried to focus attention on some of the blind spots we tend to have, and hopefully this may make your own attitude a bit less sure, a bit more tentative and open-minded.

Even with the change in our understanding of the cosmos in modern times, I make a case in this book for there being an eternal law and pattern to the Universe that is both within and outside our minds. More importantly I also tried to make the case that the Universe has a hard-wired eternal moral law. There is an awe and a wonder to that, and hopefully you can catch sight of it in a new way. When we look into

Final Thoughts

the Heavens we do not see empty expanses of space; we see eternal order, pattern and rhythm. It is alive, and we are part of it.

Saturn really makes most sense when we consider the planet as being at the border between two worlds, temporal and eternal, as are we. There are depths and dimensions to Saturn's meaning that are revealed only in that context.

And finally, I tried to bring to light and re-examine some of the difficult Saturn themes - of suffering, of evil, of pain, old age and death, aspects of life we'd just as soon look away from in our all-too-comfortable modern world. We need those hard aspects of life to be fully human, and they're not going away just because we'd like them to.

I'd like to close this book by offering you Saturnian blessings.

May you embrace your suffering. May you embrace your aging. When the time comes, may you embrace and welcome your own death. There are gifts there beyond price that can be had in to other way.

May a living awareness of the Divine, the One and the Good, the Source of All, be with you and in you in your journey, here and beyond.

Appendix

Science: the Changed Meaning of the Word

Astrology is not a science as we currently understand the word science.

For astrology to be viewed as a science we need to rethink what we mean by the word, and what that says about the world, and about what is real. Most people don't realize that **the meaning of the word science has changed drastically over the past two hundred years**. That is what I want to look at here. This involves going back into the history of our language, and recovering some of the meaning of the term Science that has been lost in the last century.

I want to give an example here of an older text where the use of science is obviously different from how we currently use the term.

The following quote is from the British Platonist Thomas Taylor, who was writing around 300 years ago. He is referring to a passage in the dialog **Parmenides** by Plato where the train of logic is using a series of negations to prove what an absolute being or God could not be – god neither exists nor does not exist. The entire train of logic is abstract and makes no reference to any empirical data.

In the late Platonist metaphysics this train of logic is taken as pointing to a conception of the One and the Good, the highest principle of things, that by definition is beyond everything we can conceive or say

Science: the Changed Meaning of the Word

about it, including saying that it has being. The quote from Taylor follows here, the emphasis in bold is mine.

> And here it must be observed that this conclusion respecting the highest principle of things, that he is perfectly ineffable and inconceivable, is the result of a most scientific series... **For that which so consistently distinguishes the philosophy of Plato from others is this, that every part of it is stamped with the character of science.**

Along with being the first person to translate all of the Platonic dialogs into English, Taylor also translated some works by the late Platonic philosopher Proclus that Taylor considered to be science in this sense of the term.

The Elements of Theology by Proclus is modeled on Euclid's elements, as is another book by Proclus that is a theological and philosophical commentary on Euclid. It is laid out as a logical and scientific argument, starting with logical axioms and building a systematic conceptual structure built on the first principles. The structure of philosophy and theology is built up as a logical and scientific structure.

The massive work by Proclus on *The Theology of Plato*, laying out the levels of the great chain of being with descriptions of the gods at each level, is similarly laid out as a closely reasoned argument that Proclus viewed as scientific – but in that work Proclus is including discussing various hierarchies of the gods. For Proclus, speaking of the Gods is a form of science.

Clearly, both Proclus and Thomas Taylor had a very different conception of science than the current meaning referring only to empirical observation and experiment. If Taylor used science in that way then that meaning must be part of the history of the English language.

Fortunately there is a way a way to recover some of that history. A very good place to start is with dictionaries. We can examine how newer

Science: the Changed Meaning of the Word

dictionaries have changed by comparing their definitions of words, with how words were defined in older dictionaries.

The 1828 *American Dictionary of the English Language* by Noah Webster is one of the most important and influential English dictionaries ever compiled, and is a masterpiece of definition, etymology, language history and usage. The Webster dictionary went through numerous changes through the years, and the last edition to preserve much of the older language meaning and usage is the 1913 edition. Almost all later dictionaries have dropped much of the earlier usage.

Both the 1828 and 1913 Webster dictionaries are available online. There is also a printed facsimile edition of the 1828 Webster available, and it is a marvelous and fascinating piece of work. Looking through the 1828 dictionary and then comparing a modern dictionary is like going from a 5 star gourmet restaurant to a MacDonald's drive-through. That is a reasonable metaphor – language in the older dictionary is so much more varied, spicy and flavorful, and language in the new dictionary is stripped down and flavorless.

When our language is stripped down, our thought is stripped down and our experience is impoverished. In the modern world we live in a fast-food reality.

As with the quote from Thomas Taylor above, these old dictionaries point to a very different world, and a very different concept of science. That is what we will examine here.

These quotes are from Webster's Revised Unabridged Dictionary (1913) – I am excerpting from the full definition of the term, which is quite long. Emphasis in bold in all quotes is mine.

> 1. Knowledge; **knowledge of principles and causes**; ascertained truth of facts.

There are two other important words here, principle and cause, both have which have changed and have shrunk in meaning over time. Firs,

Science: the Changed Meaning of the Word

the word **principle** means beginning, starting point, basis that from which everything else follows. To know the principle of something is to know its source. The word **cause** has also greatly changed and reduced in meaning over the years – in modern scientific sense of the term cause is always something physical that can be measured.

In traditional philosophy Aristotle laid out 4 different kinds of causes. Modern science has kept only the efficient cause, meaning the physical, cause and effect chain of events. Cause in the traditional sense here has connotations of Aristotle's formal cause – that which gives the shape of form – and the final cause – its end or purpose. Modern science has no place for purpose or meaning, and without that dimension astrology is meaningless.

> **If we conceive God's sight or science, before the creation, to be extended to all and every part of the world, seeing everything as it is**, . . . his science or sight from all eternity lays no necessity on anything to come to pass. –Hammond.

Just using God and science in the same sentence tells you we're living in a different world here. Link this to the concept of principle in the definition itself, and science is being used in a spiritual sense as pointing to the ultimate reality prior to the physical from which all else springs.

> Shakespeare's deep and accurate science in mental philosophy. –Coleridge.

> 2. Accumulated and established knowledge, which has been systematized and formulated with reference to the discovery of general truths or the operation of general laws; knowledge classified and made available in work, life, or the search for truth; **comprehensive, profound, or philosophical knowledge**.

> Science is . . . a complement of cognitions, **having, in point of form, the character of logical perfection,**

Science: the Changed Meaning of the Word

and in point of matter, the character of real truth. – Sir W. Hamilton.

And now we have definition number three.

> 3. Especially, such knowledge when it relates to the physical world and its phenomena, the nature, constitution, and forces of matter, the qualities and functions of living tissues, etc.; – called also {natural science}, and {physical science}.

This third definition is really the only one left in the modern dictionary. In current usage science starts and ends with measurable physical phenomena. It can be measured in a lab, it can be calculated, it can be exactly replicated in controlled circumstances – and it has no dimension of meaning, or awareness, or consciousness, or value.

A little bit later is this paragraph talking about the different dimensions of science.

> **Note: Science is applied or pure. Applied science is a knowledge of facts, events, or phenomena, as explained, accounted for, or produced, by means of powers, causes, or laws. Pure science is the knowledge of these powers, causes, or laws, considered apart, or as pure from all applications.** Both these terms have a similar and special signification when applied to the science of quantity; as, the applied and pure mathematics. Exact science is knowledge so systematized that prediction and verification, by measurement, experiment, observation, etc., are possible. The mathematical and physical sciences are called the exact sciences.

As far as I can tell we have lost half of the meaning in the modern world – science and applied science are now effectively synonyms. What Webster calls pure science has dropped out of our usage.

Science: the Changed Meaning of the Word

In this next paragraph talks about a distinctive usage of the term science which is almost the inverse of the way we currently use the term.

> Usage: {Science}, {Literature}, {Art}. Science is literally knowledge, but more usually denotes a systematic and orderly arrangement of knowledge. **In a more distinctive sense, science embraces those branches of knowledge of which the subject-matter is either ultimate principles, or facts as explained by principles or laws thus arranged in natural order.**
>
> The term literature sometimes denotes all compositions not embraced under science, but usually confined to the belles-lettres. [See {Literature}.] Art is that which depends on practice and skill in performance. "In science, scimus ut sciamus; in art, scimus ut producamus.
>
> **And, therefore, science and art may be said to be investigations of truth; but one, science, inquires for the sake of knowledge; the other, art, for the sake of production; and hence science is more concerned with the higher truths, art with the lower; and science never is engaged, as art is, in productive application.**
>
> And the most perfect state of science, therefore, will be the most high and accurate inquiry; the perfection of art will be the most apt and efficient system of rules; art always throwing itself into the form of rules." –Karslake.

In this series of paragraphs the meanings of science and art are very nearly reversed from their usage today. The 'science of ultimate principles' is gone. The other, science for 'the sake of production' is really all that is left today. The whole concept of science being 'more concerned with the higher truths' is pretty much unthinkable today.

Science: the Changed Meaning of the Word

There are no higher truths in modern science – as there is no higher world than our material world of phenomena to support such a science. **Without that higher world, astrology is meaningless superstition.** This is not just change in language but an impoverishment of our experience because we have lost the meaning of some concepts used to describe it.

I think it is very important that we become aware of just how impoverished much of our modern use of language is, and how it limits the possibilities of thinking. With the modern reduced meaning of the term, the "divine science" of astrology turns into an irrational superstitious oddity that has the connotations of words like supernatural and psychic. Astrology lies outside the modern scientific rules of what is real.

I have seen some very fine modern astrologers fall into this linguistic trap. In their eagerness to defend astrology as a "science" in the modern reductionist sense of the term, they rush to emphasize how it is important to distinguish astrology from "mere" fortune-telling or psychic arts.

Because of the lack of awareness of the change in meaning of science, I think we are using science in too narrow a sense here, and so we are discounting or missing the ways in which the practice of astrology has real affinity with psychic arts like tarot reading.

Truth in advertising disclaimer here – I read tarot and Lenormand fortune-telling cards myself, and I can't draw a hard and fast line between what I do with the cards and what I do with astrology.

In a larger sense, the practice of astrology can't exist in a linguistic and philosophical vacuum, with no system of thought to support it. We need a way of thinking about astrology that makes sense of it, and that gives it a coherent philosophical underpinning. That is the purpose of this post, and is the main theme of the current series of posts I am writing.

Science: the Changed Meaning of the Word

I now would say that astrology is indeed a science, but I am using the term in the same sense it is used by Thomas Taylor working within the Platonist tradition, as pointing to the spiritual principles, order and structure that underlies and upholds our existence in space and time. Astrology as a science may indeed have a physical dimension, but more importantly it has a spiritual and philosophical underpinning.

I do not discount the work of astrologers like David Cochrane to give astrology some empirical and statistical justification, but I do not think we can limit astrology to that realm. Astrology is too big and multi-faceted to be contained within the bounds of the modern concept of science.

If we are to be effective astrologers, and to argue our case well, we need to think clearly, we need to be clear about the meaning of the words we use – and, when we are using words like science outside of the usual connotations of the term in common discourse, we need to be very clear and explicit about that.

We are not just recovering astrology, we are also recovering a richer worldview and context within which astrology makes sense – and also recovering a divine context for our minds and our reality.

Plato and Reincarnation: the Myth of Er

Plato: The Evolutionary Journey of the Soul

Does the human soul have a purpose for being here on earth? Is our life here part of a larger experience that transcends a single human lifetime?

I come at the subject as a traditional astrologer who is rooted in the Platonic and Pythagorean tradition of philosophy.

The purpose of this essay is to examine reincarnation and the immortal soul in a Platonist model - exploring the soul's purpose in life - and how we could address it in traditional astrology.

Evolutionary Astrology

Evolutionary astrology is very popular today. It expresses a prominent dimension of modern astrology that works with reincarnation and multiple lives, and with the soul's purpose for this life within that context. This is a typically modern approach that heavily emphasizes the outer planets in talking about past lives. Like much modern astrology, evolutionary astrology typically looks to India for a metaphysical underpinning for their work.

That hunger for a sense of meaning and for a sense of soul purpose is a large part of what draws people to astrology.

Can we address the subject matter of evolutionary astrology - the soul's purpose in this lifetime viewed in the context of a series of lives for the immortal human soul - using the context and tools of traditional western astrology? Yes, I think so.

The Platonic and Pythagorean Tradition

In our own Western tradition we have a model of reincarnation, of multiple lives and an immortal soul having a purpose in this life. I look to the Platonic and Pythagorean tradition for that context.

You can make a very strong case that Plato is presenting a model of an immortal human soul that takes on a series of human lives. I realize that there is a prominent school of modern academic scholarship which claims that Plato didn't "really" believe in reincarnation or an immortal soul, and that all of the references to those in his dialogs are metaphors and not to be taken as his actual views.

In fact, there is much prominent discussion of reincarnation and the immortal soul in Plato across several dialogs, and it is stretching the "only a metaphor" argument to a point of absurdity to make his dialogs agree with the reductionist stance of much modern philosophy. Granted that the references to reincarnation and the immortal soul are not to be taken literally, they are meant to be taken seriously as pointing to an aspect of consciousness that transcends the boundaries of a single earth life.

In this post I want to examine one of the most important places where Plato presents a multi-lifetime model - the closing section of the Republic, known as **The Myth of Er.**

Note that the word myth here means account or story or tale, and does not have the modern connotations we attach to the word mythical. Plato presents it as a tale told by a warrior who has been taken for dead for some days and returns to life to share what he experienced.

I want to put the section in the context of the argument of the entire book, as this story is really the culmination.

Plato and Reincarnation: the Myth of Er

Justice leads to Happiness, Injustice to Suffering

Does it pay to act justly? Is the just life also the happy and successful life? Or, does it sometimes pay to act in unjust ways to gain advantage?

This is the question that starts the entire dialog, and is the thread that holds the entire book together. From the very start Socrates is attempting to prove that acting justly and virtuously is beneficial in its own right, acting unjustly is harmful in its own right, and that it is never of benefit to act unjustly - that acting unjustly for benefit is self-contradictory and self-defeating.

Much of the book has to do with the definition of what virtue is, and whether to act virtuously is always advantageous, or whether to act in unjust ways can produce good results. It examines justice and virtue in the context of a political structure, and in the parallel context of the individual human soul. The individual and political structures mirror each other, and virtuous action in a city is mirrored by the virtuous balance within the human soul. Both the individual and the political order are mirrors of the larger cosmic structure that we study in astrology.

The Two Worlds

In Plato's model there are two worlds, two dimensions of existence. There is the eternal world of the Forms, which transcends time and space. There is also the temporal, changing, transitory world of physical existence, of the body, the senses and passions.

There are two aspects that human consciousness that mirror these two worlds. There is the immortal soul, and there is a mortal and temporary human soul tied to the human body, and both the body and the transitory part of the soul disintegrate at death.

Both Plato and Aristotle identify the immortal soul as the *Nous*, a word that means Mind. It is the thinking, judging and reasoning part of the human. This is larger than our current concept of reason. In Plato's model reason has a connotation of underlying principles, and includes the ability to distinguish right from wrong. There is a moral and ethical dimension that is part of the basic structure of the eternal world.

The Immortal Soul

The story follows on a section [608] where Socrates attempts to prove that the soul must be immortal.

The argument for the soul's immortality is basically an argument from justice. Socrates argues that the only thing that can harm the soul is injustice or going against virtue. This means that whatever can harm or kill the body does not necessarily harm the soul.

However, acting against virtue or justice does not kill the soul, but does wound it and cause suffering. In fact the only thing that can harm the soul is acting against justice and virtue. Injustice harms the soul but does not destroy it. If the only thing that can harm the soul does not kill it, then the soul must be immortal in a just universe.

Only the physical incarnate part of us is subject to mortality, to death and destruction. Our immortal Nous, our perceiving, reasoning and judging mind, cannot be destroyed.

The basis of the Nous, the immortal soul, like the basis of the universe itself, is The Good - virtue, justice. The essence, the base principle of the universe, the One and the Good, is immortal and just - or rather, since justice emerges from the One and the Good then its source must contain and transcend justice.

In the Platonic model we live in a just universe, a moral universe, where the principles of justice reach all the way to the core of being.

This is the key principle of the entire argument - that which is real, that which eternal in the human, the immortal soul, is that part of us which makes the decisions about virtue and vice, justice and injustice. Therefore that is the part of us that is worth cultivating - and that is what the philosophic life is all about - cultivating that awareness, and learning to make it the guiding light of all of our actions.

Keep that principle in mind. We will return to it at the end of this essay, when we tie in how this dialog applies to our practice of astrology.

One Lifetime Too Short for Justice

Given that the universe is just and the human soul is immortal, it follows that each soul must have more than one mortal life, as one lifetime is too short a length of time to fully work out issues of good and evil.

This final tale, on the immortal soul, the after life, and the period between where we choose our next life, is designed to tie the entire argument together. Socrates has argued that justice is its own reward and is worthwhile in itself, and injustice is its own punishment and creates its own problems. It is never of benefit to act in an unjust way.

Now that we have that principle in place within the span of a single lifetime, the tale puts it in context of the pilgrimage of the immortal soul across multiple lifetimes, and the periods of reward or punishment between.

Note that all quotes from Plato here are from the public domain Benjamin Jowett translation, with a few sections altered for clarity by me based on the Cornford translation. Quotes are in italics, and I have emphasized some particularly important passages. The numbers in square braces are the standard section numbers for Plato's dialogs, that are referenced in all translations. For the interpretation I am particularly indebted to the translation and commentary of the Republic by F. M. Cornford.

Returning from the Dead

The transition to the story of the afterlife begins here.

Plato and Reincarnation: the Myth of Er

"Such then while he lives are the prizes, the wages, and the gifts [614a] that the just man receives from gods and men in addition to those blessings which justice herself bestowed." "And right fair and abiding rewards," he said.

Well, these," I said, **"are nothing in number and magnitude compared with those that await both after death.** And we must listen to the tale of them," said I, "in order that each may have received in full what is due to be said of him by our argument."

"Tell me," he said, [614b] "since there are not many things to which I would more gladly listen."

"It is not, let me tell you," said I, "the tale to Alcinous told that I shall unfold, but the tale of a warrior bold, Er, the son of Armenius, by race a Pamphylian.

He once upon a time was slain in battle, and when the corpses were taken up on the tenth day already decayed, was found intact, and having been brought home, at the moment of his funeral, on the twelfth day as he lay upon the pyre, revived, and **after coming to life related what, he said, he had seen in the world beyond.**

This is presented as a story told by a man who returned to life after being in the world after death. It is not described as a fairy tale or myth, but an account. How it is to be taken depends on the reader. Granted that the details may not be meant as actual description - but if it is a metaphor, then a metaphor for what? It is definitely pointing to a continued existence after death of the body, and the story at its very least is a way to point to important aspects of that existence.

If it is metaphor it definitely points to some form of continued existence over multiple lives, even if the details he frames it in here are not meant to be literal. He is pointing to it rather than pinning it down.

Plato and Reincarnation: the Myth of Er

Heaven and Hell

He said that when his soul went forth from his body he journeyed with a great company [614c] and that they came to a mysterious region where there were two openings side by side in the earth, and above and over against them in the heaven two others, and that judges were sitting between these, and that after every judgment they bade the righteous journey to the right and upwards through the heaven with tokens attached to them in front of the judgment passed upon them, and the unjust to take the road to the left and downward, they too wearing behind signs [614d] of all that had befallen them, and that when he himself drew near they told him that he must be the messenger to mankind to tell them of that other world, and they charged him to give ear and to observe everything in the place.

And so he said that here he saw, by each opening of heaven and earth, the souls departing after judgment had been passed upon them, while, by the other pair of openings, there came up from the one in the earth souls full of squalor and dust, and from the second there came down from heaven a second procession of souls clean and pure, [614e] and that those which arrived from time to time appeared to have come as it were from a long journey and gladly departed to the meadow and encamped there as at a festival, and acquaintances greeted one another, and those which came from the earth questioned the others about conditions up yonder, and those from heaven asked how it fared with those others.

And they told their stories to one another, the one lamenting [615a] and wailing as they recalled how many and how dreadful things they had suffered and seen in their journey beneath the earth - it lasted a thousand years --while those from heaven related their delights and visions of a beauty beyond words.

Plato and Reincarnation: the Myth of Er

The general argument of the Republic is that it pays to act virtuously - at the start of this section he basically says it pays off even in the context of this one life - and this tale puts it in the multi life context including a thousand years of either heaven or hell in between each life - meaning we reap tenfold of what we sow of either good or evil.

Reward or punishment after death has nothing to do with how rich, or successful, or famous, or wealthy, or well-liked, or whatever. The criteria are strictly ethical - did you live justly or unjustly. And notice it is either one or the other, completely up or completely down, an after life of unalloyed bliss or unalloyed suffering, with nothing in-between.

That argues for this being metaphorical - but then the metaphor is strongly pointing to the fact that all our actions have consequences in terms of justice and injustice - that we reap the rewards of just and virtuous action, and that we reap the suffering and ill fruit of unjust action. It is a universe where justice and injustice are core structural principles, at the very heart of what existence is all about.

What strikes me here is how very black and white dualistic it is - you are either left or right, evil or good, down or up, and there is nothing in-between. It is pretty obvious that either the Christian heaven and hell are modeled after this or they go back to a common root.

In this story, while each in-between life is either a sheer heaven or a sheer hell, between each life there is the chance to choose anew, to keep growing, to move on.

Neither condition, of either heaven or hell, is permanent. From later sections here we will see that, as within a single human life, the general human tendency is to forget quickly. Those returning from heaven tend to forget their lessons and choose poorly. Those returning from hell tend to choose more wisely since they have learned through suffering.

In terms of a single life this implies that good fortune is actually more dangerous ethically, while misfortune and suffering is the best environment for growing the soul. Or virtues grow best in a soil of adversity.

Plato and Reincarnation: the Myth of Er

Plato argues that, in general, we make our choices in life out of inertia and habit rather than conscious ethical choice. The Republic, and all of the Platonic dialogs, are arguing for conscious ethical choice as being the only thing that matters - indeed, as ultimately being the only thing that is real and eternal.

> To tell it all, Glaucon, would take all our time, but the sum, he said, was this. For all the wrongs they had ever done to anyone and all whom they had severally wronged they had paid the penalty in turn tenfold for each, and the measure of this was by periods of a hundred years each [615b] so that on the assumption that this was the length of human life the punishment might be ten times the crime;

Getting Ready for the Next Life

> ...But when seven days had elapsed for each group in the meadow, they were required to rise up on the eighth and journey on, and they came in four days to a spot whence they discerned, extended from above throughout the heaven and the earth, a straight light like a pillar, most nearly resembling the rainbow, but brighter and purer.

This plain is a place where returning souls go when they are getting ready for a new earth life - and that is the choice of each regardless of whether or not their previous place was hell or heaven.

The Spindle of Necessity

> To this they came [616c] after going forward a day's journey, and they saw there at the middle of the light the extremities of its fastenings stretched from heaven; for this light was the girdle of the heavens like the undergirders of triremes, holding together in like manner the entire revolving vault. And from the extremities was stretched the spindle of Necessity, through which all the orbits turned. Its staff and

its hook were made of adamant, and the whorl of these and other kinds was commingled.

The model that Plato describes here, which he calls the Spindle of Necessity, is the geocentric solar system, a system of spheres revolving around a spindle. From our point of view that spindle is the equator and its daily revolution - that is the clock, the main system of order that ties everything together. This is where the world of astrology comes in.

So that set of spheres around the Spindle of Necessity is the domain that the reincarnating soul enters for an earth life. That is the domain controlled by the three fates.

That implies that the larger between life domain or structure is outside of that spindle of necessity - but that the entire universe is founded, structured, on principles of justice - in other words that the very structural foundational principles or structures that the entire universe is built on, material and immaterial, spiritual and physical, eternal and temporal - is the eternal principles of justice, of beauty, of mercy and love. Literally, that without those principles the universe has no order or reason - or better yet, that without those principles there is no universe.

The spindle of necessity is the north/south pole, and the whorls or orbs are the planetary spheres plus the fixed stars. So incarnation is entering into the solar system, the world of the gods of astrology. This whole system is the sphere of the fates, and incarnation consists of descending out of the stars and through the spheres and down into earth.

> And the nature of the whorl was this: [616d] Its shape was that of those in our world, but from his description we must conceive it to be as if in one great whorl, hollow and scooped out, there lay enclosed, right through, another like it but smaller, fitting into it as boxes that fit into one another, and in like manner another, a third, and a fourth, and four others, for there were eight of the whorls in all, lying within

> one another, [616e] showing their rims as circles from above and forming the continuous back of a single whorl about the shaft, which was driven home through the middle of the eighth.
>
> And the spindle turned on the knees of Necessity, and up above on each of the rims of the circles a Siren stood, borne around in its revolution and uttering one sound, one note, and from all the eight there was the concord of a single harmony.

The music of the spheres - all of the planetary rotations together sounding a harmony.

The Three Fates

> And there were another three [617c] who sat round about at equal intervals, each one on her throne, the Fates, 1 daughters of Necessity, clad in white vestments with filleted heads, Lachesis, and Clotho, and Atropos, who sang in unison with the music of the Sirens, Lachesis singing the things that were, Clotho the things that are, and Atropos the things that are to be.

These are the three Fates - so they are outside of the entire system, not to be identified with any one planet. And also, the domain of the Fates is life on earth - and a bit later in this section it is made clear that *each soul freely chooses* its coming lifetime - either thoughtlessly or thoughtfully.

The fates are those powers that structure the world of past, present and future - that weave the web and pattern that makes up the incarnate human existence that we know.

One way or other it is chosen in terms of desire and value - the soul gets the life it is lusting after.

And Clotho with the touch of her right hand helped to turn the outer circumference of the spindle, pausing from time to time. Atropos with her left hand in like manner helped to turn the inner circles, and Lachesis [617d] alternately with either hand lent a hand to each.

"Now when they arrived they were straight-way bidden to go before Lachesis, and then a certain prophet first marshaled them in orderly intervals, and thereupon took from the lap of Lachesis lots and patterns of lives and went up to a lofty platform and spoke,

'This is the word of Lachesis, the maiden daughter of Necessity, "Souls that live for a day, now is the beginning of another cycle of mortal generation where birth is the beacon of death. [617e] No divinity shall cast lots for you, but you shall choose your own deity. **Let him to whom falls the first lot first select a life to which he shall cleave of necessity.**

But virtue has no master over her, and each shall have more or less of her as he honors her or does her despite. The blame is his who chooses: God is blameless. "

Our Life is Our Responsibility - There is no Blame

Each soul chooses its lot in life, the general shape of the life it wants and the challenges it gets. God is blameless; each is responsible for their own lot. Essentially this means that we choose our own fate.

We choose our lives in terms of what we value, and we reap the consequences of those value choices. Essentially we choose what we want out of the life; we then reap the consequences of those choices.

So saying, the prophet flung the lots out among them all, and each took up the lot that fell by his side, except himself;

> him they did not permit . And whoever took up a lot saw plainly what number he had drawn.
>
> [618a] And after this again the prophet placed the patterns of lives before them on the ground, far more numerous than the assembly. They were of every variety, for there were lives of all kinds of animals and all sorts of human lives, for there were tyrannies among them, some uninterrupted till the end and others destroyed midway and issuing in penuries and exiles and beggaries; and there were lives of men of repute for their forms and beauty and bodily strength otherwise [618b] and prowess and the high birth and the virtues of their ancestors, and others of ill repute in the same things, and similarly of women.
>
> But there was no determination of the quality of soul, because the choice of a different life inevitably determined a different character.

Very important here - the good or bad fortune of the life has nothing to do with the determination of quality of soul. That means good or bad fortune can be turned to good or bad account according to justice and virtue. (This is very important in astrology when we work with the benefics and malefics, the planets of good and ill fortune. Benefic and malefic has nothing to do with good and evil in any ethical sense.)

At a higher dimension, this implies that there is an already planned set of lives to be chosen from, to be enacted. This implies that each human life has a place. Life is structured like a play where the main plot and its characters are set, and now the actors are all selecting their part within the play.

> But all other things were commingled with one another and with wealth and poverty and sickness and health and the intermediate conditions. - And there, dear Glaucon, it appears, is the supreme hazard for a man.

Plato and Reincarnation: the Myth of Er

> [618c] And this is the chief reason why it should be our main concern that each of us, neglecting all other studies, should seek after and study this thing - **if in any way he may be able to learn of and discover the man who will give him the ability and the knowledge to distinguish the life that is good from that which is bad, and always and everywhere to choose the best that the conditions allow**, and, taking into account all the things of which we have spoken and estimating the effect on the goodness of his life of their conjunction or their severance, to know how beauty commingled with poverty or wealth and combined with [618d] **what habit of soul operates for good or for evil,**

It is worth emphasizing that good and bad fortune, and good and evil, are two completely different categories. We do not have control over the general shape of fortune once we get here - in this model we have already previously chosen our lot in life - but we always have control over quality of soul, over good and evil response - and it is precisely that response which determines how we are judged.

> and what are the effects of high and low birth and private station and office and strength and weakness and quickness of apprehension and dullness and all similar natural and acquired habits of the soul, when blended and combined with one another,

> so that with consideration of all these things he will be able to make a reasoned choice between the better and the worse life, [618e] with his eyes fixed on the nature of his soul, naming the worse life that which will tend to make it more unjust and the better that which will make it more just.

This is the core - the main argument of the Republic - and the main reason for human life - is to grow in our ability to make conscious and wise value judgments.

Plato and Reincarnation: the Myth of Er

But all other considerations he will dismiss, for we have seen that this is the best choice, [619a] both for life and death. And a man must take with him to the house of death an adamantine faith in this, that even there he may be undazzled by riches and similar trumpery, and may not precipitate himself into tyrannies and similar doings and so work many evils past cure and suffer still greater himself, but may know how always to choose in such things the life that is seated in the mean and shun the excess in either direction, both in this world so far as may be and in all the life to come; [619b] for this is the greatest happiness for man.

"And at that time also the messenger from that other world reported that the prophet spoke thus: **'Even for him who comes forward last, if he make his choice wisely and live strenuously, there is reserved an acceptable life, no evil one. Let not the foremost in the choice be heedless nor the last be discouraged.'**

When the prophet had thus spoken he said that the drawer of the first lot at once sprang to seize the greatest tyranny, and that in his folly and greed he chose it [619c] without sufficient examination, and failed to observe that it involved the fate of eating his own children, and other horrors, **and that when he inspected it at leisure he beat his breast and bewailed his choice, not abiding by the forewarning of the prophet.**

For he did not blame himself for his woes, but fortune and the gods and anything except himself.

He was one of those who had come down from heaven, a man who had lived in a well-ordered polity in his former existence, [619d] participating in virtue by habit and not by philosophy; and one may perhaps say that a majority of those who were thus caught were of the company that had come from heaven, inasmuch as they were unexercised in suffering. But the most of those who came up from the earth, since they had themselves suffered and seen the sufferings of others, did not make their choice precipitately.

For which reason also there was an interchange of good and evil for most of the souls, as well as because of the chances of the lot.

Choice from Inertia

This is one of the most interesting twists of the whole story - those who had just come from hell were more likely to make good choices, and those from heaven more likely to make foolish choices! The good don't keep getting gooder, and the bad don't keep getting badder. Part of the lesson seems to be precisely that point, that good and bad fortune do not coincide with good and evil, and that we can take bad fortune in this life and turn it towards goodness of soul.

> **Yet if at each return to the life of this world [619e] a man loved wisdom sanely,** and the lot of his choice did not fall out among the last, we may venture to affirm, from what was reported thence, that not only will he be happy here but that the path of his journey thither and the return to this world will not be underground and rough but smooth and through the heavens.
>
> For he said that it was a sight worth seeing to observe how the several souls selected their lives. [620a] He said it was a strange, pitiful, and ridiculous spectacle, as the choice was determined for the most part by the habits of their former lives.

How slow we are to learn from experience! Even in terms of soul growth we are mostly creatures of simple habit. Again the emphasis on living consciously here and now, that what we are ultimately building

Plato and Reincarnation: the Myth of Er

is character and quality of soul, and that any life circumstance can be used to contribute to that growth.

> And it fell out that the soul of Odysseus drew the last lot of all and came to make its choice, and, from memory of its former toils having flung away ambition, went about for a long time in quest of the life of an ordinary citizen who minded his own business, and with difficulty found it lying in some corner disregarded by the others, [620d] and upon seeing it said that it would have done the same had it drawn the first lot, and chose it gladly.
>
> And in like manner, of the other beasts some entered into men and into one another, the unjust into wild creatures, the just transformed to tame, and there was every kind of mixture and combination.
>
> But when, to conclude, all the souls had chosen their lives in the order of their lots, they were marshaled and went before Lachesis. And she sent with each, [620e] as the guardian of his life and the fulfiller of his choice, the genius that he had chosen, and this divinity led the soul first to Clotho, under her hand and her turning of the spindle to ratify the destiny of his lot and choice; and after contact with her the genius again led the soul to the spinning of Atropos to make the web of its destiny irreversible, and then without a backward look it passed beneath the throne of Necessity.
>
> [621a] And after it had passed through that, when the others also had passed, they all journeyed to the Plain of Oblivion, through a terrible and stifling heat, for it was bare of trees and all plants, and there they camped at eventide by the River of Forgetfulness, whose waters no vessel can contain.
>
> They were all required to drink a measure of the water, and those who were not saved by their good sense drank more than the measure, and each one as he drank forgot all things.

Plato and Reincarnation: the Myth of Er

Each are required to drink the water of forgetfulness - but the wise ones drink less - implying that it is thirst for experience that keeps driving us here - and also implying that wisdom keeps in mind that the life we are living is our own choice - is a mirror of our desires and values - basically that we get the life that we choose, that we want.

We learn by living out our desires and values, learning from them. As we grow and mature over the lives our values grow and mature, and mere earthly desire or good or bad fortune become left behind, and true soul or spiritual growth is left as the real good, the only real value. The growth process over multiple lives parallels the growth process in a single well-lived human lifetime.

> [621b] And after they had fallen asleep and it was the middle of the night, there was a sound of thunder and a quaking of the earth, and they were suddenly wafted thence, one this way, one that, upward to their birth like shooting star.
>
> Er himself, he said, was not allowed to drink of the water, yet how and in what way he returned to the body he said he did not know, but suddenly recovering his sight he saw himself at dawn lying on the funeral pyre.
>
> - And so, Glaucon, the tale was saved, as the saying is, and was not lost.
>
> [621c] And it will save us if we believe it, and we shall safely cross the River of Lethe, and keep our soul unspotted from the world.
>
> **But if you will believe with me that the soul is immortal and capable of enduring all extremes of good and evil, and so we shall hold ever to the upward way and pursue justice with wisdom** always and ever, that we may be dear to ourselves and to the gods both during our sojourn here and when we receive our reward, [621d] as the victors in the games go about to gather

in theirs. And thus both here and in that journey of a thousand years, whereof I have told you, we shall fare well.

Here ends the Myth of Er, and the Republic.

We reap what we sow in terms of good and evil, so growth through the lives is growth in righteousness and wisdom - the two are synonyms.

Conclusions

Here are the general conclusions that are drawn in the Republic, and in the Platonic tradition in general.

As human beings we have immortal souls - or better, we are immortal conscious beings currently living mortal lives. We don't HAVE souls, we ARE souls.

The part of us which is immortal is what Platonists would view as the rational part. I think that reason as we currently think of it has too limited a connotation. I think of it as the part of us that makes conscious and ethical decisions. It is also the part of us that can stand back from our mortal condition and judge how to act.

Given that the soul is immortal, this means that we grow and evolve through a series of lives. The part of our lives that survives this one life is our ethical and moral part, and concerns our acting with justice or injustice. It is the part that makes value judgments.

The basic shape of our lives is chosen by us according to what we desire - we choose the basic shape of our lives. This means that we are here in this particular life condition because there is a set of experiences we have chosen for a specific purpose. This purpose is both for us as individuals, and for us as part of the larger human collective - we are growing, changing, and evolving, individually and collectively.

The life we choose aligns with our values and desires, and our choices can be more or less thoughtful, reasoned and conscious. As in any single event in our lives, our choices and actions may be careful and thought out, or thoughtless and impulsive. The Myth of Er story specifically describes someone jumping into a life without thought and then bewailing their choice, blaming the Gods, blaming fate - blaming anything except themselves.

It follows that a central part of the overall purpose of human life is precisely this growth process, learning the implications and consequences of our desires and values. Like children growing into adults, our desires and needs grow and change. Our sense of values and our conduct changes and matures as we have more experience and (hopefully but not necessarily) become more self-aware - though I would say that lack of self-awareness can be viewed as younger or more immature, and developed self-awareness can be viewed as more advanced or mature.

This growth in awareness of values is a meta-value to the entire process that spans lives - self-awareness, choosing our values maturely, deliberately, rationally and consciously.

This is where the path of philosophy comes in, as being a path of self-awareness - and this is also where astrology comes in.

What of Astrology?

How does this tie in with astrology?

Astrology only makes sense in the context of the philosophic life. To me this means that astrology needs to include growth in awareness of value judgments. Most people I work with are less concerned with what will happen to them, and more concerned with the Why questions, questions of purpose and meaning.

Given that there is a purpose to human life, the question then becomes how we can best work with, and respond to, the lot in life that we are cast, in such a way as to further our growth in virtue and self-awareness. This benefits us, it benefits others and it benefits our society. Ultimately, in a way beyond we can usually conceive, our life fits within a larger cosmic order.

This concept of the multiple levels of order all mirroring each other is one of the foundation principles of the Republic. Individual human virtue is mirrored in a virtuous structure in the political arena, and this in turn is a mirror of the cosmic order of the heavens. We study astrology to align ourselves with cosmic order, which includes a moral order.

How does astrology help? By helping us to wake up, to engage in this process of growth in values consciously by thinking through our desires and values so that we may choose and act more wisely.

This is the purpose of astrology - to help us to make wise and self-aware choices of how to live our lives, and to take responsibility for those choices.

Recall from the story that it is the Fates who offer us the lives from which to choose, and it is the Fates who weave and control the structure and unfolding of that fate through a life within Plato's Spindle of Necessity - life on earth surrounded by the heavens, the whole cosmic structure mirrored in astrology.

The movement and order of the planets in astrology shows the unfolding of that order - or, in other terms, our fate. We always need to remember that fate does NOT determine whether we choose to act justly or unjustly - that is always within our choice - and sometimes that is all that is within our choice.

This growth in awareness over time and experience leads to the conclusion that is the central premise of the entire Republic dialog. Simply put, it is wise to act righteously and unselfishly, and it is unwise to act selfishly and dishonestly. In the larger multi-lifetime view of things, virtue pays and vice punishes - and ultimately that is all that matters. The only truly important things in life are those concerned with the state and growth of our immortal souls.

Plato and Reincarnation: the Myth of Er

This assumes there is a built in moral order to the universe - that existence is not morally neutral - and, that the underlying structure of the universe is one of justice. Justice is not some kind of overlay that we place as humans on top of a morally neutral material universe. The structure of justice is wired right into the very basic principles on which all of creation is built. In Platonic terms, justice is one of the primary platonic forms - or in other terms, justice is one of the most basic and primary of the gods.

The One and the Good - moral goodness, justice, fairness, mercy, are properties of our universe that are so foundational that they precede and underlay even existence itself. We are part of that Oneness, and part of our purpose here is to wake up to that fact, and to always act within that context.

Bibliography

Addey, Tim, *Beyond the Shadows: The Metaphysics of the Platonic Tradition*. Westbury, Prometheus Trust, 2011.

_____, *The Unfolding Wings: The Way of Perfection in the Platonic Tradition*. Westbury, Prometheus Trust, 2011.

Al-Biruni, *The Book of Instructions in the Elements of the Art of Astrology*. Bel Air MD, Astrology Classics, 2006.

Aquinas, Thomas, Ed. by Peter Kreeft. *Summa of the Summa*. San Francisco, Ignatius Press, 1990.

Butler, Renn, *Pathways to Wholeness: Archetypal Astrology and the Transpersonal Journey*. London, Muswill Hill Press, 2014.

Bonatti, Guido, *Book of Astronomy, Treatise 3*. Translated by Benjamin N. Dykes, PhD, Minneapolis, Cazimi Press, 2010.

Carter, Charles E O, *The Principles of Astrology*. Wheaton, Ill, Quest Books, 1963.

Chesterton, Gilbert Keith, *Orthodoxy*. San Francisco, Ignatius Press, 1986.

_____, *The Thing: Why I am a Catholic*. San Francisco, Ignatius Press, 1990.

Cochrane, David, *Astrology for the 21st Century*. Gainsville Fla, Cosmic Patterns Software, Inc., 2002.

Davison, Ronald C. *Astrology: The Classic Guide to Understanding Your Horoscope*. Sebastopol, CRCS, 1987.

Dobyns, Zipporah, Ph. D., *The Book of Saturn*. ,San Diego, ACS Publications, 1996.

Bibliography

Alighieri, Dante, *Convivio*, Book Two chapter 13, the Richard Lansing translation. It is available online at this url. https://digitaldante.columbia.edu/text/library/the-convivio/book-02/.

Dykes, Benjamin N. Ph. D, *Introductions to Traditional Astrology: Abu Ma'shar and al-Qabisi*. Minneapolis, Cazimi Press, 2010.

Ebertin, Reinhold, *The Combination of Stellar Influences*. Tempe AZ, AFA, 1940.

Efrein, Laurie, *How to Rectify a Birth Chart*. Wellingborough, Aquarian Press, 1987.

Firmicus Maternus, Julius, *Mathesis*. Translated by James H. Holden. Tempe, AFA, 2011.

Forrest, Steven, *The Inner Sky: The Dynamic New Astrology for Everyone*. San Diego, ACS, 1988.

George, Llewellyn, *A to Z Horoscope Maker and Delineator*. St. Paul, Llewellyn Publications, 1977.

Greene, Liz, *Saturn: A New Look at an Old Devil*. York Beach, Weiser, 1976.

Heindel, Max, *The Message of the Stars*. Oceanside CA, Rosicrucian Fellowship, 1998.

Hickey, Isabel M. *Astrology: A Cosmic Science*. Sebastopol CA, CRCS, 1992.

Hillman, James, *On Senex Consciousness*. In Maxwell and Grant, *Saturn*, 2016.

Holden, James Herschel, M.A., *Biographical Dictionary of Western Astrologers*. Tempe AZ, AFA, 2012.

Ibn-Ezra, Avraham, *The Beginning of Wisdom*. Translated by Meira Epstein. ARHAT, 1998.

Bibliography

Lewis, C.S., *The Abolition of Man*. New York, Harper Collins, 1974.

_____, *The Discarded Image: An Introduction to Medieval and Renaissance Literature*. United Kingdom, Cambridge University Press, 2013.

Lilly, William, *Christian Astrology*. Edited by David Roell, Bel Air MD, Astrology Classics, 2004.
(A pdf facsimile of the original Christian Astrology is available at the following url: https://archive.org/details/ChristianAstrologyByWilliamLilly/page/n1. The excellent Astrology Classics edition referenced above has modernized some of the spelling and English usage.)

March, Marion, and McEvers, Joan, *The Only Way to Learn Astrology. Volume 1, Basic Principles*. San Diego, ACS, 1970.

Maxwell, Grant and Tarnas, Becca, Editors, *Saturn and the Theoretical Foundations of an Emerging Discipline*. Nashville, Persistent Press, 2016.

Plato, *The Laws*. Translated by Thomas Taylor and Floyer Sydenham. In *The Works of Plato, Volume II*. Westbury, Prometheus Trust, 1996.

Plato, *The Republic*. Translated by Thomas Taylor and Floyer Sydenham. Kshetra Books, 2016.

Plato, *The Republic*. Translated by Benjamin Jowett. Public Domain, available online.

Raphael, *The Key and Guide to Astrology*. New Delhi, India, Sagar Publications, 1970.

Rudhyar, Dane, *The Practice of Astrology As a Technique in Human Understanding*. New York, Penguin, 1968.

Bibliography

Ruperti, Alexander, *Cycles of Becoming: The Planetary Pattern of Growth*. Sebastopol, CA, CRCS, 1978

Sepharial, *The Manual of Astrology*. London, W. Foulsham and Co., 1979.

Shaw, Gregory, *Theurgy and the Soul: The Neoplatonism of Iamblichus*. University Park, Pennsylvania State University Press, 1995.

Valens, Vettius, *Anthology*. Translated by Mark Riley. Available online at:
http://www.csus.edu/indiv/r/rileymt/Vettius%20Valens%20entire.pdf.

Witte, Alfred, LeFefeldt, Hermann, Rudolph, Ludwig, *Rules for Planetary Pictures: The Astrology of Tomorrow*. Westview FL, Penelope Publications, 1990.

www.ingramcontent.com/pod-product-compliance
Lightning Source LLC
Chambersburg PA
CBHW020647300426
44112CB00007B/268